JUMPERS FOR GOALPOSTS

HOW FOOTBALL SOLD ITS SOUL

ROB SMYTH & GEORGINA TURNER

First published 2011 by Elliott and Thompson Limited
27 John Street, London WC1N 2BX
www.eandtbooks.com

ISBN: 978 1 907642 22 7

This edition published in 2011

9 8 7 6 5 4 3 2 1

A CIP catalogue record for this book is available from
the British Library.

Printed and bound by CPI Group (UK) Ltd, Croydon, CR0 4YY
Typset by Envydesign Ltd.

For our Dads

CONTENTS

HOW FOOTBALL SOLD ITS SOUL

O f course, you'll have to *define* the soul of football, they said. Balls.

Orange ones, on snow covered pitches. That's the sort of image that springs up as the mind casts around for the essence of the game we fell in love with before anyone knew better. The sort of stuff Julie Andrews could have sung a song about, while chucking small children under the chin. It's virtually impossible to grasp the notion of football's soul tightly enough to hold it still, yet lightly enough to appreciate its contours and colours in your hands. We were certain, though, that we could assemble a team whose attributes combined to do some of the explaining for us, a sort of Soul of Football XI. We have laid the team out in a loose 2-3-5 formation. This is absolutely because of our belief in the innocent charm of such a formation, and has nothing to do with the fact that most of the natural choices were midfielders and attackers. Ahem. We're also conscious that most of the players included are British or Anglicised; we're not xenophobes, honest.

COACH: CESAR LUIS MENOTTI

BERT TRAUTMANN

DAVE MACKAY   **JOHN CHARLES**

DANNY BLANCHFLOWER   **ROY KEANE**   **SOCRATES**

STANLEY MATTHEWS MATT LE TISSIER KENNY DALGLISH BOBBY ROBSON LIONEL MESSI

Bert Trautmann

Physical courage has always been an enormous part of football, whether it's Diego Maradona repeatedly demanding possession despite the chilling menace of some of the most malevolent swine ever to roam the green, or people who have played on with broken arms, collarbones and legs. But the Manchester City goalkeeper Bert Trautmann took that to a whole new level when he played in an FA Cup final with a broken neck. A *broken* neck. A broken *neck*. *A broken bloody neck!* It's the single most jaw-dropping act of bravery in football, and fitting for a man who covered the full spectrum of courage. When he arrived at Manchester City in 1949, having grown up in Hitler's Germany and been part of the *Luftwaffe*, over 20,000 protested at his signing. Trautmann won them over with his heroism, his decency – he actively sought out Manchester's Jewish community to discuss his background – and, of course, his brilliance in goal. Matt Busby told his Manchester United players never to look up when they played against Trautmann; the moment he caught their eyes, he would decipher precisely what they were planning to do.

2

Dave Mackay

Mackay is the incarnation of the strong, silent type. He was a player who went about his business without fanfare or melodrama; who simply got on with his job because it was, well, his job. Even when he suffered serious injury he would barely react. Mackay's courage was exceptional by any standards, and he was the sort of leader to whom a crowd could relate and aspire: a man of iron will but also dignity and fairness. He upheld the unspoken code of honour between footballers: that they would compete with rare intensity, but that they would never cheat or attempt to injure each other. A lament for the potential extinction of Mackay's type applies not just to football but to masculinity itself.

John Charles

A giant of the game in every respect, Charles was known as *Il Gigante Buono (The Gentle Giant)* during his time at Juventus. He was a tough man but scrupulously fair, never being booked or sent off during his career. During his first Turin derby, in 1957, Charles collided with a defender as he was about to shoot; when the defender collapsed to the floor, Charles eschewed a one-on-one and put the ball out of play.'I only had the goalie to beat but it didn't seem fair,' said Charles. 'I put the ball out for a shy so the fella could be looked after.' That night he heard tooting outside his villa, and saw a number of Torino fans waving scarves. He asked them what was going on, and was told that they wanted to thank him, so Charles invited them in –'about 20 all told, and by the time they left in the early hours of the morning they had drunk all my wine.' It was a typical gesture from one of sport's true gentlemen. 'John wasn't only one of the greatest footballers who ever lived,' said Sir

Bobby Robson. 'He was one of the greatest men ever to play the game.'

Danny Blanchflower

Blanchflower, captain of Spurs' legendary Double-winning side of 1960/61, embodies the fading belief that glory is more important than victory, and that the way you do something is more important than what you do. 'The great fallacy is that the game is first and last about winning. It's nothing of the kind. The game is about glory,' he said. 'It's about doing things in style, with a flourish; it's about going out to beat the other lot, not waiting for them to die of boredom.' Blanchflower, a tactical visionary, also had no interest in the extraneous ego-massage that football offered: he became the first person to turn down the chance to appear on *This Is Your Life*, imperiously walking away from Eamonn Andrews live on air. He also refused to compromise his punditry during a spell in America, when he was told to be positive rather than honest for fear of offending. The gentleman was never for turning.

Roy Keane

Those who remember Keane's appalling, indefensible challenge on Alf-Inge Haaland, not to mention his furious haranguing of team-mates and opponents, might legitimately dispute his inclusion in a Soul of Football XI. Yet Keane is an almost uniquely complex character, and other sides of his multi-faceted persona are very much in keeping with the themes of this book. The most important is his searing honesty, so utterly refreshing in a sport increasingly defined by disingenuousness. It was that, as much as anything, that made his 2002 autobiography one of the greats of its genre. Other admirable elements of Keane's nature include the forensic intelligence he brings to his work; the fact he cares about football sufficiently to rage so furiously against the dying of its light; his peerless bullshit detector; his rejection of the corporate and celebrity cultures that surround modern football; and his lyrical capacity to sum those up in a pithy phrase, as he did with talk of prawn sandwiches and Rolex culture.

Sócrates

There are very few jobs as cool as that of the professional footballer, and so it seems like a fair trade to ask in return that our footballers should be cool – yet so few are these days. There is certainly nobody to compare to Sócrates, the effortlessly chic Brazilian who captained their wonderful 1982 and 1986 World Cup sides. Sócrates looked the part, with a languorous gait and a big, enviable beard. Even the sweat patch on his Topper shirt, the result of the fierce heat during the Mexico World Cup, somehow looked good. He soaked his shirts even though he was not exactly the most vigorous of footballers: Sócrates preferred the art of football, passing the ball rhythmically around the field. Not trying too hard was the essence of his cool, too: there was no posturing and very little ostentatiousness (we'll forgive him showy penalties in 1986). He was a heavy smoker and drinker during his playing days, is a doctor of medicine and one of the smartest men to play the game. As with everything else, he wore intelligence lightly. It's one of the many reasons that he was the coolest of them all.

Stanley Matthews

It's hard to find many greater examples of commitment to football than a man playing at the top level in his fifties. Sir

Stanley Matthews did just that for Stoke in 1965, the culmination of an incomparable 33-year career that was testament to his athleticism and dedication: Matthews was a near-vegetarian teetotaller in an age when meat and pints were jostling with oxygen for importance. In some respects it is uncomfortable to see someone sacrifice so much of their life in the name of a sport; equally, however, it reflects an admirable devotion to the game. Matthews was occasionally accused of excessive individualism, but essentially he was a selfless man, with his role as one of football's first great facilitators reflecting his humility and also his focus on team rather than individual success. Glory would come to him through other means than the scoresheet: his dazzling wing-play in the 1953 FA Cup final led to it being christened the Matthews final, even though he scored none of the goals in Blackpool's 4–3 win over Bolton.

Matt Le Tissier

Le Tissier played eight times for England. He did not win a single trophy in his career. Yet he will be remembered more vividly and more fondly than 99% of the players who won more caps or medals. Le Tissier was loved up and down the country, not just by his disciples at Southampton. That was mainly because of his sublime talent, which enabled him to have his own Goal of the Season competition most years, but there was more to it than that. Le Tissier's loyalty to Southampton, where he never earned more than a basic wage of £3,900, showed that simple happiness was more important than money and murderous ambition. He loved being at Southampton, so why should he leave? If that suggested a rounded attitude to life, then his rounded figure was also part of Le Tissier's charm. In his autobiography he says that, during his playing days, his principal vice was not women, drugs, alcohol or gambling, but a Bargain Bucket from KFC. Once he ate so many Sausage & Egg McMuffins on the way to training that he had a fainting fit. He was just a normal bloke with an abnormal genius, the kind of footballer we all wanted to be.

Kenny Dalglish

With loyalty becoming an archaic concept in football, it's inevitable that we're drawn to those who have an enduring and spiritual relationship with their club. Few, if any such relationships as are powerful as the one between Kenny Dalglish and Liverpool. It has been built upon rich success – Dalglish has won 19 trophies as a player and manager at Anfield – but also tragedy, at Heysel and Hillsborough. The latter, which came during Dalglish's time as manager, hit him so hard that he eventually resigned almost two years later, still struggling to cope with the aftermath. Dalglish was an established world star when he joined Liverpool at the age of 26, yet he instinctively understood the club's values – both at the time he arrived, and particularly when they were shaped by subsequent tragedy. He may have been adopted by the club, but the bond between the two is stronger than most biological relationships.

Bobby Robson

It's often said that, if the world were full of the same type of character, it would be a pretty boring place. But we'd take a world full of Sir Bobbys. What a serene, happy place it would be. If there has been a nicer man involved in football, as player or manager, then we haven't come across him. The extent of Robson's decency was such that it almost brought a lump to the throat; one of the most telling things about his popularity was that, after his death in 2009, the usual naff, bad-taste jokes that fly around social media were conspicuous by their absence. Just as Robson was loved by the football family, so he had an unconditional love for everything about the game that often transcended any partisan concerns. When his England side drew 2–2 away to a thrilling young Denmark side in 1982, Robson said: 'It would have been a travesty of justice if we had won. Denmark were brilliant. I did not see many better teams in the World Cup finals. We were overrun in midfield by a team who did not have a single bad player.' Such generosity of spirit marked Robson out as unique. He was the definition of the phrase 'a football man', somebody who was steeped in and obsessed with the game. 'In my 23 years working in England,' said Sir Alex Ferguson, 'there is not a person I would put an inch above him.'

Lionel Messi

He is the best player in the world, perhaps the best player of all time, yet Lionel Messi still oozes the same humble *joie de football* of a little kid playing in the park. This is apparent not just in his wondrous self-expression with the ball, but also in his goal celebrations. For Messi there is no choreography or affectations of cool, just a delirious charge of celebration, his little head usually bobbing with delight. Such childlike enthusiasm is increasingly rare, but then Messi is a throwback in more ways than one: his general disinclination to dive or complain to referees is in complete contrast to the prevailing ethos, both in football and specifically at his club Barcelona. He has the simple enthusiasm of the boy who wants to be Diego Maradona or Lionel Messi. The fact that he *is* Lionel Messi hasn't changed that one bit.

Manager: César Luis Menotti

There are two main reasons why César Luis Menotti would coach our Soul of Football XI. One is his commitment to playing football with style. The controversy over certain refereeing decisions during Argentina's triumphant 1978 World Cup campaign, and the occasionally alleged fix against Peru, sometimes obscures the thrilling, futuristic, high-speed football that they played. The other reason is that Menotti is the most impossibly cool manager of all. As he patrolled the touchline during that World Cup campaign, Menotti took drags on cigarettes that were thinner than a bookie's biro, exuding a sophistication that was thrilling and other-worldly. It is hard to find that level of mystery at the World Cup now, but the memories of Menotti – and the likes of Josimar and Salvatore Schillaci – live on: in his *Guardian* text commentary on the 2010 World Cup final, Scott Murray went on a memorable Menotti riff. 'I like to picture him sitting in one of these spherical white plastic chairs, fag and long G&T on the go, bossa nova on the stereo, idly flicking through some socialist literature as he glances out of his apartment window over the River Plate, while beautiful women breeze past him in long billowing chiffon dresses, occasionally catching his eye.'

* * *

Not all of the dream team above embody all of football's elementary qualities, and some of them might not even get along all that well (the smell of fried chicken emanating from Le Tissier's pores would've made him a difficult room-mate for Matthews, anyway), but collectively they produce something approaching a definition of football's soul. In its purest form, football is a game of glory and honour, played by players prepared to dedicate themselves to it – Le Tissier always said that if he'd needed to, he would have improved his diet and application to stay in the team; the beautiful thing was that it was never necessary. Football doesn't require superhuman musculature and a set of lungs that could service a horse, but it demands a sense of style, of fair play and of good, honest competition. 'There were plenty of fellers who would kick your bollocks off,' said Bolton and England striker Nat Lofthouse, who scored the winner against Austria in 1952 despite various assaults en route. 'The difference was that at the end they'd shake your hand and help you look for them.' At its best, soccer elicits an unfathomable sense of loyalty and affinity, to the exclusion of avarice and (for the most part) self-regard. A well-contested game of football has the power to grab you by the amygdala and shake an unconscious chortle out of you regardless of your allegiance to a crest. If that all sounds hopelessly idealistic, well, good: all is as it should be. 'The human soul has still greater need of the ideal than of the real,' said the 19th century French thinker Victor Hugo (we've read some proper books for this). 'It is by the real that we exist; it is by the ideal that we live.' If you look modern football hard in the face, you can't help but notice it's dead behind the eyes.

There is no single point at which it all went wrong – though Messi is the only current player on the list, the Soul of Football XI is far from a collection of obscure faces peering out of grainy pictures on a Pathé newsreel – but history generally demands staging posts, and for that purpose, 1992 is football's *annus ridiculus*. It's the year that the European Cup became the Champions League, and the year that British football – with which most of this book is concerned – was made an indecent proposal, and accepted; we're not far off the point where Sky is actually paying £1 million a night.

It's important, for context, that we start at the beginning; there have been arguments about money ever since the Football Association allowed clubs to pay professionals in 1885 – in fact the decision only came about because clubs such as Preston North End were already paying players, and didn't much like being turfed out of competitions on account of it. Some of the figures from the pre-maximum wage era are quite revealing, suggesting as they do a long-standing tendency towards inflationary pay for footballers: before the FA imposed a £4 per week limit for the 1901/02 season, some players were earning three times the average wage before bonuses. Even the maximum wage was twice what manual workers earned in a week, but that didn't stop almost constant wrangling and wrestling for power. Players complained of being slaves – 'the professional footballer's contract is an evil document,' according to Len Shackleton – under the retain-and-transfer system, which meant they were quite literally the property of the club they signed for.[1] Generally, however, there was a sense of perspective, however grudging. The nomadic Tommy Lawton must have fallen out with every chairman he met, such was his gall at the proportion of a club's earnings spent on players' wages, but he acknowledged that, 'In comparison with the average working man, you were doing very well. What we earned was a fortune compared to the man in the street.'

The efforts of the Football League – often hamfisted, but

---

[1] It's interesting in the context of everything else written here that the player registration system was so restricted by the Football League because certain clubs had already begun to use their financial muscle to attract the best players. *'That's what I do' said the scorpion.*

usually motivated by a concern for the health of the league as a whole – came unstuck in 1961, when the players threatened a strike if the maximum wage (by then £20 per week) wasn't lifted. Its abolition had an instant impact, not least because Fulham chairman Tommy Trinder had rather carelessly insisted that he would pay Johnny Haynes £100 per week if only he could, and Haynes took the cuttings to his office quick-smart. At that stage, all Football League clubs were still bound by an agreement to share gate receipts equally between the home side and their visitors, but the threat of a breakaway league formed of the wealthiest clubs saw that go out of the window in 1981, followed not too far behind by the four per cent gate levy that was equally shared between the league's 92 clubs. In 1983, the then Tottenham Hotspur chairman Irving Scholar floated the club on the London Stock Exchange, a first in sport. Soon 50 per cent of the centrally negotiated television money was going to the top flight, too. Following the Hillsborough disaster in 1989, clubs were paying more attention than ever to stadium conditions, getting ready to welcome a new, gentrified football audience turned on by Italia '90. Struggling for satellite converts, Rupert Murdoch looked out of the window and saw the perfect storm breaking. Within the next 20 years, Sky would put more than £6 billion into English football.

Living the dream
In the summer of 1992, as in the winter of 2010/11, Kenny Dalglish decided to invest a British record fee in a hugely promising but unproven Geordie centre forward. In 1992, Alan Shearer was about to turn 22 and had scored 43 goals in 158 games for Southampton. Nineteen years later, Andy

Carroll had just turned 22 and had scored 33 goals in 91 games for Newcastle and Preston. Two very similar cases, then, with one major difference: the fee. Shearer cost £3.3 million, Carroll £35 million. Inflation is a bitch? That level of inflation is more of a femme fatale; £3.3 million in 1992 would have been worth £5.2 million 19 years on.

Seven months after Carroll's move, the 2011 summer window closed with Premier League clubs having spent £485 million on player transfers – up 33% on the previous summer,[2] and more than double the spend in 2003. That was the year the January transfer window was introduced, during the first of which Premier League clubs spent £35 million; in 2011, they spent £225 million. The unique nature of English football –'muck and bullets', as Roy Keane called it – and the need for homegrown players to comply with UEFA rules mean that transfer fees are particularly extreme for English players and, to a lesser extent, foreigners who have Premier League experience. Carroll had one England cap, as did Jordan Henderson when he went from Sunderland to Liverpool for £16 million. Phil Jones was uncapped, and had played only 31 Premier League games, when he left Blackburn to join Manchester United for £16.5 million. Inflation in the football transfer market has been so dramatic that some famous splurges of the past are completely dwarfed. The Liverpool manager Kenny Dalglish (his wallet fattened by Chelsea's £50 million spend on Fernando Torres) spent £80 million on four British players in 2011 – Henderson, Carroll, Stewart Downing (£20 million) and Charlie Adam (£9 million); when he created arguably Liverpool's greatest team

---

[2] Gross spending in the top tiers of leagues in Italy, Spain and France was also up on the 2010 figures. Bundesliga clubs spent about the same year on year.

by purchasing John Barnes, Peter Beardsley, John Aldridge and Ray Houghton in 1987, he spent £5.5 million. And when Dalglish supposedly bought the title for Blackburn eight years later (a dubious claim, in truth, even at the time), he spent £25 million over three seasons. Even Real Madrid's first *galactico* period seems fairly tame by modern standards: they spent around £280 million in six years.

All of this is set against a backdrop of global economic turmoil and the return to the everyday lexicon of 'austerity'; in Britain public services are subject to endless nips and tucks to keep costs down and the £50 million paid by Chelsea for Torres is roughly equivalent to the NHS Trust budget cuts that threatened hospital closures around the same time. It's that kind of comparison that encourages such revulsion, but the spending levels in modern football would look crass even in more prosperous times. 'Clearly there is a point at which it becomes in anybody's mind ridiculous,' the Premier League chief executive Richard Scudamore said after the Torres deal went through, 'but I don't think we're at that level.'

Best not to dwell too long on wondering what 'that level' might be; the revenue figures in football are already beyond mind-boggling. Deloitte's 2011 Review of Football Finance stated that, in the 2009/10 season, the combined revenues of the five big European Leagues – England, France, Germany, Italy and Spain – amounted to €8.4 billion (up by five per cent); of that, €2.5 billion was generated in the Premier League, in excess of €800 million more than the (more profitable) German Bundesliga and more than three times as much as the English top flight posted in 1996/97. La Liga in Spain saw the biggest leap in figures between the 2010 and 2011 reviews, thanks primarily to the seemingly ever-increasing earning potential of Barcelona and Real Madrid.

Barcelona were always supposed to have a bit more integrity than to get involved in the scramble for money, as is implied in their 'More Than A Club' philosophy. They went without any sponsorship on their shirts for 107 years. Then, when they did have a sponsor, it was Unicef, with Barcelona paying €1.5 million a year to the charity. It seemed a perfect and heartwarming response to the commercial desperation on show elsewhere, but it was nothing of the sort. Once the fans were accustomed to having a sponsor's logo on the Barcelona shirt, the club could more comfortably sell the space. Even more absurdly, for a club that prides itself on its independence and representation of Catalonia, the name on their shirt is that of another country, Qatar, paying Barcelona €166 million over five years. It's not just shirts that are for sale. In the summer of 2011, Manchester City sold the naming rights to their stadium to Etihad for over £400 million. It may seem unthinkable that Camp Nou, the Bernabéu or Old Trafford would be up for sale, but the same was true of Barcelona having shirt sponsorship. When City signed their deal, their then chief executive Garry Cook described it as 'one of the most important arrangements in the history of world football'.

In the past, an important football arrangement was something like Rivelino-Gerson-Clodoaldo-Jairzinho-Pelé-Tostão. Increasingly, however, the actual football is secondary to off-field business. In the last 25 years, business has become such an integral part of football, particularly English football, that it's hard to know where one ends and the other begins. Football's *raison d'être* has changed so thoroughly that at least as much energy is spent figuring out ways to exploit commercial opportunities as holes in the opposition back four. If that seems melodramatic, take a look at the

Manchester United badge. The words 'football club' were removed in 1998; it can't be that long before a crest is designed with 'PLC' stitched into it. The increased importance of money has nuked any notion of fair competition. It is almost impossible to succeed in England, Italy, Spain and the Champions League without spending huge sums of money on players and their wages. When Manchester City won the FA Cup in 2011, they had spent £400 million on transfers in the previous three years and pushed their wage bill up to £133 million; at the start of the 2011/12 season it was reported that they were paying out a quarter of a million pounds a week to players who were no longer in manager Roberto Mancini's plans – some of them weren't even at the club, but having their wages elsewhere subsidised by City.

The scale of these figures gives them shock value (momentarily, anyway), but City aren't alone, of course. The wage bill at Chelsea was highest in 2009/10, at £172 million; the total wage bill for the 20 Premier League clubs was £1.4 billion (an all-time high wages-to-revenue ratio of 68%). In 1991–92, the last season before the Premier League, that figure was £54 million – that's an increase of 2493% in 19 years.[3] 'You're looking at being a top-four team and it's difficult,' said the Tottenham manager, Harry Redknapp, in 2011. 'We can't pay the wages that [the top four] clubs pay, basically.' There is invariably a distinct correlation between the final league table and the transfer league table, and an even stronger correlation between the league table and the wages table, with Arsenal being the honourable exception in

[3] The perception that this kind of spending is little more than the corporate equivalent of a giddy, guilty payday binge is strongly reinforced by the fact that the biggest spikes in wages occurred in 1997/98, 2000/02 and 2007/08 – straight after new TV deals were signed.

terms of transfer fees, if not wages. Still, two of their three Premier League titles under Arsène Wenger – in 1998 and 2002 – came after major spending the previous summer (the manager's reticence in the transfer market was exposed to fierce scrutiny when the 2010/11 campaign unravelled so drastically after defeat in the League Cup final in the February, precipitating a £51 million spend in the summer).

Real Madrid and Barcelona both have a heftier wage bill than the famously generous New York Yankees baseball team. In a survey of the highest paid athletes in 182 countries, 114 were footballers, with 36 of them playing in England (where the best paid *Englishman* was actually the Formula One driver Lewis Hamilton). Neil Webb, a classy midfield player who won 26 England caps and would have had a lot more but for a devastating Achilles injury in 1989, at the age of 26, had to work as a postman when he retired. It's hard to imagine that Frank Lampard, Steven Gerrard or even a one-cap wonder like Lee Bowyer will be delivering your mail in years to come. You would have to be incredibly inept or vice-ridden to find ways to blow the wages most footballers earn – though that's not to say a few of them don't manage it.

Managers, too, earn startling amounts. Fabio Capello topped the *FourFourTwo* 2010/11 managerial Rich List, with an estimated wealth of £36 million, and nobody has parted fools and their money more successfully than Sven-Göran Eriksson. During the 2010 World Cup he earned a reported £22,000 a day as coach of the Ivory Coast. 'I don't think I am paid that well,' he deadpanned. By the time he stepped down as England manager in 2006, he was earning £4.5 million a year. The salary epitomised English football's buy-now-pay-later philosophy – a culture that developed around the turn of the century, when all manner of managers had licence to spend all manner of fees on all manner of dross. Matías Vuoso (£3.5 million), Seth Johnson (£7 million), Corrado Grabbi (£6.75 million), Juan Pablo Angel (£9.5 million), Boško Balaban (£6 million), Steve Marlet (£13.5 million), Ade Akinbiyi (£5 million), Nicolás Medina (£3.5 million, played one game). The list was almost endless.

The thought of how much agents made in such moves is enough to make you shudder. Despite the questions raised by relationships between agents, players and club representatives in several high-profile moves in the noughties (including Ashley Cole's transfer from Arsenal to Chelsea), the game's various governing bodies never seem to have total jurisdiction over agents' roles in football. There appears to be ample scope for an agent's self-interest to dictate things – Samir Nasri's agent Jean-Pierre Bernès was talking to journalists about 'what direction Samir wants to take with his career' even while the player was discussing a contract extension with Arsenal. In the two years to October 2010, Premier League clubs paid £137 million in fees to agents who brought their clients in to negotiate a transfer elsewhere or even simply to renegotiate their existing contracts; in total, 13% of money spent in English professional football is spent on agents. Chelsea spent just under £19 million on agents in that time, despite signing only three new players.

At the other end of the spectrum, Blackpool paid out around £45,000 – because they insist that the players pay their agents themselves. The Seasiders' then chief executive Karl Oyston said: 'I don't think any deal should be about the agent. It should be about the player, about giving them a platform to perform on one of world's best stages. Agents are sometimes denying their clients that chance.' It wouldn't be fair to say that agents are bad people, but their influence on football does evoke Larry David's discussion of a friend with Hodgkin's disease: 'I said he had the good Hodgkin's, I didn't say it was a *great* Hodgkin's.' 'I see so many of them happy to sow division if it means they get a better deal, often working against the interests of clubs, players and supporters,' wrote the former Crystal Palace chairman Simon Jordan. 'And yet the game still opens its arms and embraces them. It's a problem on both sides: agents out to bleed the game dry supposedly in their client's best interests, and egotistical, irresponsible officials who are more than happy to roll over and let them.'

In the modern era, the recklessness of clubs keen to get on in football's upper reaches is astonishing. The rise and fall of Leeds United ought to have been a fable. Between the summer of 1999 and January 2002, they spent around £90 million on players – not much now, but an immense sum then. Especially as they couldn't afford it. When they reached the Champions League semi-final in 2001, their chairman Peter Ridsdale said they were 'living the dream', but the dream turned out to be of the David Lynch variety. Leeds overreached so badly (Ridsdale left behind debts of £78 million) that they ended up in desperate financial trouble and were relegated within three years of that semi-final appearance in Valencia. Following their £90 million spree, Leeds spent under £10 million in almost 10 years. In 2008, Lord Triesman, then the FA chairman, suggested that the total debt in English football was close to three billion, and that such 'toxic debt' caused 'very tangible dangers' to the game, at all levels. In the first 19 years of the Premier League, 54 clubs in the Football League became insolvent, and by 2011, the average Championship club was spending

£4 for every £3 generated in its quest to land a top flight payday. Clubs at all points of the spectrum have got themselves into an almighty financial mess. At the last count, Manchester United's debt stood at roughly £590 million; in the summer of 2011, Barcelona – Barcelona! – banned colour photocopies at the club so as to save money. They can afford to bid £40 million for Cesc Fàbregas and pay an average salary of £5 million, but woe betide anyone who dares to ask for a colour printout.

Onwards

In 2004, Simon Jordan described football as a 'bullshit world' full of 'bullshit people' – and perhaps the best that can be said in response is that it is an improvement on the verdict of *The Sunday Times* in the 1980s: 'a slum sport played in slum stadiums and increasingly watched by slum people'. But with merit increasingly redundant and money now waving the conductor's baton in double time, even Jordan's assessment looks kind. There is so much wrong with modern football that you could, er, fill a book.

In the chapters that follow we take various aspects of the contemporary game – players, managers, competitions, those in higher authority, supporters and the media – and size them up against football's past and its ideals, considering how and why change has come about and, eventually, how different kinds of change might be initiated. Plenty of the cultural shifts and schisms we talk about get us into a right royal funk (how *did* we get to the point where Charlie Brooker could liken idolising a footballer to worshipping a shire horse, and you kind of got what he meant?) and at some points nostalgia – bald, irrational pining – has slipped past the editors, but it's mostly quite well considered, and occasionally factually correct. It might be a lament, but it's not a moan. We don't hate football. We're just not sure we want to buy what it's selling.

CHAPTER 1

FALSE IDOLS

'The responsibility on the sportsman is heavy. Once he has attracted hero worship he constantly has to conduct himself, on and off the field, in a way that presents youngsters with an example.'

– Duncan Edwards

Nobody scrutinised masculinity like Tony Soprano. He interrogated it furiously, desperately, even irrationally, yearning to understand why modern man had lost the plot. Much of this was the projection of internal frustration; as *padrino* of television's favourite mob family, Tony Soprano was the ultimate example of the tortured angst that exists in the middle of the Venn diagram that has 20th-century man to the left and 21st-century man to the right. But while he was far from perfect, he at least had an idea of what masculinity should represent – even if he was tantalisingly unable to achieve it.

A recurring theme in *The Sopranos* was Tony's lament to his psychiatrist, Dr Melfi: 'Whatever happened to Gary Cooper? The strong, silent type.' We might well ask the same of football. Once it was full of strong, silent types: Obdulio Varela, who captained Uruguay to World Cup victory in 1950 and had a strength of will to compare with that of Keyser Söze; Danny Blanchflower, who led Spurs to the double in 1961; Bryan Robson, Manchester United's longest-serving captain who bore a grotesque series of injuries without complaint or self-pity, to name a few – dignified men who quietly got on with their work. Dave Mackay is perhaps the best example of the strong, silent type so commonplace in football's past. Mackay was the definitive man's man, and definitely one of the good guys, an outstanding left-half who was at the heart of the most successful spells in Hearts', Tottenham's and Derby's histories, and a truly honourable man. He used his clout to put the hurt on opponents but never – never – to seriously hurt them. 'Mackay was unquestionably the hardest man I ever played against,' said George Best. 'And certainly the bravest.' After suffering a grotesque leg-break at Old Trafford in 1963, which would keep him out for almost two years, Mackay barely grimaced. As he was stretchered off he sat up leaning on his elbow, looking almost bored.

Mackay was a bona fide hero, the likes of which are increasingly rare in football. To some this will seem a piddling point, but it's quite the opposite. When American psychologist Abraham Maslow was working on his theory of human motivation in the 1940s (go with it, this almost works), he came up with a hierarchy of needs, at the tip of which was what he called 'self-actualisation'. 'What a man can be, he must be,' Maslow wrote. 'This need we may call self-actualisation… it refers to the desire for self-fulfilment, namely, to the tendency for him to become actualised in what he is potentially. This tendency might be phrased as the desire to… become everything that one is capable of becoming.' Maslow didn't mention heroes directly, but they're an implicit part of the process: role models supply invaluable life lessons, idealise certain behaviours, and shape our ambitions – help to shape, that is, what we believe and hope we are capable of becoming. For the sake of avoiding an embarrassing tête-à-tête with outraged psychologists in our local Wetherspoon's, we should add that Maslow would probably expect the properly self-actualised person to eventually transcend these role models, and focus first and foremost on his/her own strengths and weaknesses. But you get the point: Bonnie Tyler isn't the only one holding out for a hero.

This stuff doesn't stop being important once you've solemnly removed the last page of *SHOOT* from your bedroom wall, put all your worldly possessions into the back of a Renault 5 and left home; fans of all ages invest a staggering amount of time and emotion in their team, the men they consider heroes. When you consider how much bronze has gone into immortalising yesterday's heroes – Johnny Haynes and Bobby Moore stand over sculpted footballs on opposite sides of London, Billy Wright looms large as life outside Molineux, Tom Finney lunges towards the ball in a Deepdale fountain; the list goes on – it's nonsense to say that as adults and cynics we don't care about the cut of a man's jib. When Blackpool unveiled a gigantic 9 ft statue of Jimmy Armfield in May 2011, manager Ian Holloway joked that 'there can't be any bronze left in the world', but called it 'a proud moment for everybody at the club' and added: 'I've given them some half-decent players who might in 40 years' time be revered themselves.'

It's not a complicated recipe – take a great and dedicated player, bake in the heat of fans' adoration for a few decades, ready plinth – but Holloway's appreciation for its essential ingredients is disappointingly rare in a world where Manchester United winger Nani reportedly hangs his medals on the life-size marble sculpture of himself that stands in the middle of his living room. Just as words like 'celebrity' have rapidly depreciated thanks to giddy overuse, the currency of the football 'hero' has suffered the effects of quantitative easing – the modern habit of clubs celebrating any half-decent footballer as a hero, no matter how incongruous the label and his conduct. Even half-decent is optional. 'New hero shirts now available online, get kitted out today!' said the email from Nottingham Forest, in the opening weeks of the 2011/12 campaign; upon clicking open, the recipient was confronted with pictures of journeymen summer signings Andy Reid, Jonathan Greening and George Boateng. Perhaps one day this trio will join Brian Clough, hands raised in victory, as bronze fixtures in Nottingham's Market Square, but it seems unlikely. Stuart Pearce doesn't have so much as a plaque, yet.

Heroism should be in the eye of the beholder, not the Big I Am. But as the marketing machine shudders up through the gears, supporters have been forced to relinquish naming rights. And not just to the megastore: increasingly, the players are happy to deify themselves, settling for the warm and unfailing glow of self-regard. 'I have vanity, yes,' Ronaldinho once said. 'I'm vain. But only within normal limits.' An endearing admission, or at least it would have been had he not said it at the launch of his own range of clothing, which included a T-shirt of the Virgin Mary wearing a Ronaldinho shirt.

* * *

During his 1990s assault on celebrity culture, Paul Kaye creation Dennis Pennis battled his way to the front of the media scrum surrounding *Some Like It Hot* actor Tony Curtis, ageing gracefully on the arm of a pneumatic blonde, at a film premiere. 'My name's Dennis, man,' he explained, having caught Curtis' eye. 'I specialise in making celebrities look ridiculous… but I don't think I'll bother this time.' Immediately spinning on his heel, Pennis leaves the date stifling a giggle while Curtis struggles to fix a recovery stare on the middle distance.

Anyone for Pennis? A worrying number of modern footballers, their eyesight ruined by all those hours looking at the mirror, seem to need a heads up. In 2001, Newcastle forward Carl Cort was ejected from a supermarket after his former wife allegedly pulled the 'Don't you know who I am?' trick while trying to jump the queue. (As it transpired, even Cort's own manager, Sir Bobby Robson, didn't know who he was. Asked what Robson called him, Cort's teammate Shola Ameobi replied: 'Carl Cort'.) When the Köln goalkeeper Faryd Mondragón was dropped halfway through the 2010/11 season, he said, 'I feel as if I have a knife in the back… Jesus was betrayed and deceived, too.' Then there's El Hadji Diouf, a constant source of inadvertent entertainment. 'You can't talk about Senegal without talking about El Hadji Diouf,' he said. And referring to himself in the third person isn't the worst of it: 'It's like if you wanted to understand the history of France without speaking of Charles de Gaulle.' Who hasn't at some stage made the obvious connection between one of history's most important figures and a bloke who had a half-decent World Cup before eventually playing for Bolton and Blackburn?

Not that a bulging trophy cabinet does much for the modern footballer's charm. More often than not, they exhibit the voluble self-satisfaction of self-made millionaires rather than people who took a lucky dip in the gene pool; Tony Soprano would clench his fists on sight of 99% of them. Many modern footballers are winners; very few are heroes. And the saddest thing is that most of them wouldn't know the difference. To contrast Mackay and his brethren with the majority of current footballers is to make chalk and cheese seem like siblings, twins even. After a goalless draw with Denmark in 2004, Italy's players complained – wearing earnest expressions – that their socks had ruined everything. 'The thread that these socks were made with is too rough,' said Christian Panucci.

In one respect, that is simply a reflection of the changes in masculinity evident in wider society – but football offers an extreme, condensed version of that process. If the game was once about understated masculinity, now it is about lurid machismo. Today's players are still obsessed with assertions of masculinity, mind. With Chelsea's top-four status in danger in spring 2011, John Terry announced that it was time for his teammates to 'man up'. During Euro 2004, the now-retired Italian striker Christian Vieri told the Italian press that 'none of you may judge me as a man because I am more of a man than all of you put together. You have no idea how much of a man I am.' Safe to say they had a better idea after that outburst. Masculinity as embodied by the modern footballer is not so much strong and silent as weak and gobby, players so mollycoddled by clubs and agents that they strut around high on testosterone yet barely able to function independently (Alain Goma famously phoned Fulham's player liaison officer in a panic because his fish were swimming in the wrong direction).

No one expects footballers to be perfect, or even *that close* – football is more than familiar with the troubled hero; in George Best it had one of the world's most famous examples. The most interesting human beings are invariably those who are significantly flawed. It's as much a question of panache as anything. Best announced himself at 19 years old with an astonishing performance away to Benfica in the 1966 European Cup quarter-final second leg, and for a long while his precocious talent and easy charisma combined with tales of drunken debauchery to make him a rock star as much as a footballer. When Best quipped: 'I spent a lot of money on booze, birds and fast cars. The rest I just squandered,' men and women alike sighed dreamily. We were utterly charmed by Best, and the likes of Stan Bowles, Rodney Marsh and Charlie George, because for all their faults – childish/dangerous/licentious/other – they breathed the same life into the game as the Stones and the Beatles did into the charts.

Their lives were at times far removed from our own, but their demeanour was enthralling rather than alienating. 'Lamps', 'Becks', 'JT', 'Stevie G', 'Wazza'… today's footballers sound more like the manufactured pop bands chasing fame and fortune on the newsstand, where *OK!* magazine pays for wedding pictures and tabloids tell the sordid tales of one-night stands. When *EastEnders* actress Barbara Windsor recalled, many years later, sleeping with George Best, she said: 'He was so beautiful. He came over to me and I said, "Don't waste your time with me darling, you've got all these lovely ladies after you." And he said, "When do I ever get to talk to somebody like you?" That was it; that did it. A magic moment.' No one would argue that Best wasn't thinking with one hand on the buckle of his belt, but he at least took the trouble to cast a little spell – the one man in the room who probably didn't need to.

Today's players seem to assume that any woman within a 50 ft radius is simply in the queue. When hairdresser Aimee Walton alleged a one-night stand with Ashley Cole, she told the *Sun*: 'Ashley was already drunk and couldn't keep his eyes off me, but he wouldn't come and chat... At the end of the night one of his mates just came up to me and said, "Ashley wants you to go home with him."...He slapped my backside so hard his wedding ring left an imprint.'

EXCESS 1-0 SUCCESS

Billy Bremner was not, by any stretch of the imagination, the perfect footballer. His temper was filthy and his tackle often filthier; caught by Bremner on his return from a second leg-break in 1966, Dave Mackay took the Leeds midfielder up by the scruff of the neck and unleashed a nuclear glare; 'I called him a dirty little bastard.' Bremner was banned for 11 games after a punch-up with Liverpool's Kevin Keegan during the 1974 Charity Shield, and a year later he was banned for life from international football after getting chucked out of a Copenhagen nightclub and boozily wrecking his hotel room after Scotland had beaten Denmark 1–0. Yet Brian Clough, who hated Leeds United, agreed with Bill Shankly that Bremner was one of the greats, and once wrote in his programme notes: 'To Leeds United, Billy Bremner is as priceless as a work of art.' Today the first thing away supporters see as they approach the turnstiles at Elland Road is a statue of Bremner that is carefully repainted every couple of years. He was and is adored beyond comparison with his teammates or even his manager, Don Revie. The fact that he chain-smoked, drank and gambled on card games made him a flawed athlete and role model, but it also made him just like the fans. He was *their* dirty little bastard.

The bond between fans and players has never been more strained than it is 30 years after he hung up his boots. The changes in the archetypal footballer's lifestyle have made it nigh on impossible for fans to relate to them. As part of their coverage of the 2006 World Cup, ITV ran a competition to win a footballer's life. This did not entail training at Stamford Bridge, running out at Anfield, not even getting the hairdryer. The prizes were a £28,000 Cadillac, a week in the Hotel Martinez in Cannes and a day on a yacht. Not a football in sight.

In the old days you had every chance of seeing your favourite player in the local pub on a Saturday night; since the narcissistic nineties and noughties, there has been no way past the velvet ropes of the VIP area. In May 2011, a brawl at West Ham's end-of-season party allegedly started because Demba Ba, who denied the claim, couldn't be bothered to sign an autograph. Whatever actually happened, the event itself highlighted the 24-carat gulf that has opened up between supporters and their teams. Fans paid £275 each to attend, while players were warned they would be fined a week's wages if they didn't. Even at the end of a relegation season, the club felt that cash bribes might be necessary to get their players to show their faces for a couple of hours. The episode couldn't help but call to mind the brilliantly complex

Joey Barton's reaction to the slew of autobiographies from England players after the World Cup in 2006. 'Why were they bringing books out?' he asked, not unreasonably pointing out that England had exited the competition in the quarter-final, having lit few fires along the way. As he put it, '"we played like shit, here's my book".'

Barton sets himself apart from football's gentrification generation, which has access to a previously unimaginable lifestyle and renown, and which is never better symbolised than by David Beckham. Beckham largely seems like a decent chap (and he's a notable exception when it comes to supporters, never failing to applaud them at the final whistle), but he arguably represents both the pinnacle and the nadir of the modern cult of the celebrity footballer. Beckham is the handsome offspring of football's love affair with money: blond, grinning, wearing a few squirts of Intimately Beckham, and still the richest footballer in the world. Even as he moved beyond his mid-30s, managers at some of Europe's most ambitious clubs drooled at the thought of adding his name to their squad list, like the writers of *Coronation Street* securing a George Clooney cameo. As the journalist Simon Moon wrote in 2006, Beckham's 'name is as instantly recognisable as that of multinational companies like Coca-Cola and IBM'. As long ago as March 2000 – before he had even worn his first sarong in public – Beckham was a significant part of a course in football culture at Staffordshire University. (The course leader said that Beckham had a 'fair degree' of ability, which, while probably underrating an excellent player, indicated that football celebrity would now have little to do with his ability.)

Money defines the modern footballer to such a degree

that in 2011, one Premier League coach was rumoured to be leaving his club because he no longer felt he could get through to the players, such is their fixation on money to the exclusion of everything else. In the past, you could judge a player's career by saying, 'Show us yer medals'; now they are more likely to put their payslips on the mantelpiece. The wages that players receive are mind-blowing. According to Futebol Finance's 2011 figures, Real Madrid pay Cristiano Ronaldo £883,000 a month, while Barcelona pay Lionel Messi £772,500. This is all before endorsements and sponsorship deals. Nineteen of the world's 50 best-paid players are in the Premier League, where Fernando Torres and Yaya Touré's annual salaries are listed at £8.8 million. None of the other 17 earns less than £4.7 million a year. Manchester City defender Wayne Bridge – at No. 20 on the Premier League earnings list – spent the second half of the 2010/11 season on loan at West Ham, who got relegated. He was banking £367,000 a month. Though wages outside of football's upper echelons are inevitably less obscene, even players in the lower leagues can take home as much in a month as most nurses would in a year. During a spectacular Twitter meltdown in September 2010 (in which he also said the club had given him two Mercedes cars as a signing-on fee), former Rushden & Diamonds striker Leon Knight posted a picture of his bonus: £30,000 in cash stuffed inside a Tesco bag.

Footballers fought an ongoing battle over wages in the past. By the time Jimmy Hill (then chairman of the footballers' union) started arguing for the abolition of the maximum wage in the 1950s, the best-paid players earned up to £5 a week more than the average person in the stands. As most people's wages had more than quadrupled since the

1930s, Hill argued that they could afford to dig a bit deeper at the gate and thus fund higher wages. The Football League agreed that the limit should be raised, but they wanted to keep a ceiling in place; Hill, arguing that players' values were already being determined by market forces in the advertising world (where Bobby Charlton was the face of... the Flour Advisory Bureau), wanted football wages to be a free market, and won with the help of a strike threat in 1961. As rising wages later started to generate more comment, Sir Stanley Matthews (an irrefutable hero) said: 'People say the wages are too high, but it's a short career.' Then, well before the first £200,000 a week deal, it was a valid point, and one that was leant credence by the sad stories of World Cup winners such as George Cohen selling their medals to fund their retirement. At least Robbie Fowler, who's now playing in the Thai Premier League, invested much of his Premier League wealth in a property portfolio that would see him in pipes and slippers for years to come (and gave Liverpool fans the chance to sing, to the tune of 'Yellow Submarine', 'we all live in a Robbie Fowler house').

Wages have now, however, gone far beyond such defences, and the ways in which they are discussed belie not a concern for pension plans but simply for more. Matt Le Tissier retired in 2002 having never earned a basic rate above £3,900 per week at Southampton, the club he stayed at for 16 years despite the wealth and medals he might have earned elsewhere. 'I've no regrets whatsoever,' he said, when asked if his loyalty had been worth the sacrifice. 'I had an ambition to be a professional footballer and I had an ambition to play for England, and I did both at Southampton.' It's not as if Le Tissier missed the Premier League boat, and this puts the infamous passage in Ashley Cole's 2008 autobiography, in which he expressed his disgust at being offered a mere £55,000 a week by Arsenal, into perspective:

> When I heard Jonathan Barnett [Cole's agent] repeat the figure of £55K, I nearly swerved off the road. 'He [former Arsenal Director David Dein] is taking the piss, Jonathan!' I yelled down the phone. I was so incensed. I was trembling with anger. I couldn't believe what I'd heard.

Nor could we believe what we had read. In one respect Cole had a point – as a world-class player, England's most consistent at the very highest level in roughly the last 20 years, he was entitled to expect a higher wage relative to his Arsenal teammates. It was the manner in which he complained that tweaked our sensibilities, indicative as it was of the way in which so many modern footballers had long since lost reality's contact details. Not many fans forking out for tickets at the Emirates would mind David Dein taking the piss at that price.

Occasionally this craven regard for money gives us moments of delightful schadenfreude – as in 2008, when the Manchester City forward Darius Vassell was mugged of £23,000 worth of bling while he was arguing over a cab fare. Most often, though, it produces tales of grim excess. It is in man's nature to be frivolous with money, but some of the stories we hear about Premier League footballers are astonishing. At the end of the 2010/11 season, a report in the *Sun* claimed that the Manchester City forward Mario Balotelli had accumulated £10,000 in parking fines in under a year. Staff, it was said, had to rescue Balotelli's car 27 times. 'Mario doesn't seem to care,' said a Manchester City source in the same report. 'It's a drop in the ocean to him. Mario was pulled over by the police and he had £25,000 cash on the passenger seat. They asked him why and he said, "Because I can".'

The startlingly eccentric Balotelli is not really representative of all footballers but such monetary excess is far from unique to him. Stephen Ireland once spent £260,000 on a customised Bentley for his girlfriend – complete with red leather seats into which was stitched: 'To Jess Love From Stephen.' And to think we once laughed at his black Range Rover with pink trim. Still, at least he got some mileage out of them – one Premier League player tells the story of being in a taxi with a former teammate, a longstanding England international, who threw a £40,000 watch out the window simply to show off. There are umpteen tales of Premier League footballers either burning money or throwing a wad of notes straight up in the air and laughing at the resulting free-for-all. Football's milieu has changed from Hovis advert to Bret Easton Ellis novel, a life of pomp and ceremony in which excess trumps success, and WAGs and wages are compared like ornate business cards.

Even players' more mundane investments demonstrate a similar detachment from or disregard for the realities of ordinary life. In 2008, Steven Gerrard spent – and you'll like this – £350,000 on a two-storey gym on the site of a former bungalow next door to his house in Freshfield. The gym is so big that it has a separate postcode to Gerrard's house. He won planning permission despite complaints from locals, one of whom said it was 'like building an Asda supermarket in the middle of a beauty spot'. A number of footballers seem to have taken interior design tips from the film *Scarface* – no surprise, given that most of them name Oliver Stone's tale of the Miami coke wars' savagery and excess as their favourite movie. Gerrard's former Liverpool teammate, Harry Kewell, had a plasma TV in every room of his house, including two in the bathroom so that he and his wife could both watch while they were in the bath. That bath weighed a tonne, and required ten men and a crane just to get it into the house. It makes Gary Neville's hedgerow, shaped into the letters MUFC, and his brother Phil's 'P&J' woven carpets, seem r ather tame.

DON'T YOU WANT ME, BABY?

In this boundless onanistic orgy of reward and self-regard, the oft-repeated cliché that 'no player is bigger than the club' has lost its currency. For supporters, a club's story and traditions, highs and lows, are often interwoven with their own, and in the past they shared genuine emotional ties with star players. Today they're well advised not to expect footballers to really 'get' what they're a part of, or be anything more than indifferent to any narrative bigger than their own. In Martin Cloake and Adam Powley's collection of stories from Spurs fans, *We Are Tottenham*, DJ Norman Jay tells the tale of a phone call he received from one of the players following a 4–0 defeat to Chelsea in the FA Cup in 2002.'"I'm having a party in a couple of weeks, I hope you can do it," all bright and breezy,' Jay recalled. 'And I thought, "you fucking tosser. You've just been stuffed 4–0 and you're thinking about having a party".' Never mind being bothered about the result himself, it hadn't even occurred to the player that a fan's mood might be darkened by the defeat. The relationship between players and the game has become increasingly dysfunctional in the past couple of decades; there are three people in this marriage, and the third is money. She's a pushy and divisive mistress.

Until the Bosman ruling of 1995, players were only able to transfer when their clubs said so. In 1990 Jean-Marc Bosman was struggling to get a game having reached the end of his contract at RFC Liège, yet found the club was knocking back transfer offers from elsewhere – and they cut his wages, to boot. So he took them to court. Five years later the European Court of Justice decided that players should have the freedom to leave a club (for anywhere in the EU) at the end of their contracts, without a transfer fee being due. While the case all but ruined Bosman, he empowered players in a quite unprecedented way.

It's not that we might begrudge Joe Cole his £4.7 million-a-year Bosman move to Liverpool in 2010, really, but once in sight of the end of their contract, 'negotiations' are now horrendously skewed in the players' favour: my way or the bye-bye way. In October 2010 Wayne Rooney refused to sign a new deal because, he said, Manchester United were in decline. Stories circulated that he'd be prepared to see out the 18 months left on his contract and sign for Manchester City, a cross-town transfer that might actually have stopped the earth spinning on its axis, at least for a moment. Two days later he signed a new, double-your-money £200,000-a-week, five-year deal with United; Sir Alex Ferguson was alternately hailed as a master of persuasion and a complete mug. Either way, the signs are that players seem to think they have their clubs by the balls – later that year, Ajax striker Mounir El Hamdaoui reacted to being named on the bench for a Champions League match against Milan by phoning in sick every day for more than a month. In response Ajax fined him, before demoting him to the reserves for a further misdemeanour, but couldn't shift him off the books because he demanded terms no other clubs would agree to. (Ajax actually gave his shirt number to new signing Dmitri Bulykin regardless, but suffice to say, the relationship between players and clubs seems a bit off these days.)

Have a look at the starting line-ups from the 1966 World Cup final and the 2010 World Cup last-16 match between England and Germany:

ENGLAND 1966	ENGLAND 2010
Banks, G.	James, D.
Cohen, G.	Johnson, G.
Charlton, J.	Terry, J. (c)
Moore, B. (c)	Upson, M.
Wilson, R.	Cole, A.
Stiles, N.	Milner, J.
Ball, A.	Lampard, F.
Charlton, B.	Barry, G.
Peters, M.	Gerrard, S.
Hurst, G.	Defoe, J.
Hunt, R.	Rooney, W.

If we exclude reserve teams and loan periods, the 1966 World Cup winners had played for, on average, 1.3 teams apiece. Fast forward to 2010 and the statistic stands at 2.8 teams – doubled and then some. And while at an average age of 29, the 2010 team had been playing for a little longer than the 1966 team (which averaged 26 years), it seems pretty unlikely that a side with eight – yes, eight – single-club men in the line-up, would squeeze in a further 1.5 teams in a three-year period. No one had played for more than two different teams in 1966. By comparison, the 2010 side boasts only two one-club players, John Terry and Steven Gerrard – and they've both enjoyed high-profile flirtations with other clubs. The pattern is the same for the Germans, even if it's slightly less pronounced. On average, the 1966 World Cup runners-up had played for 1.7 teams; five of them were one-club men and only one player (Karl-Heinz Schnellinger) had played for more than two teams. In 2010, the average age of the team – 25 – hadn't changed, but the clubs average stood at 2.2. Three players had turned out for only one club: Bastian Schweinsteiger, Thomas Müller and Sami Khedira (who transferred from VfB Stuttgart to Real Madrid immediately after the World Cup).

'The nearest thing to true unconditional love is that of a lad for his football team.' So wrote *United We Stand*'s Steve Black in the early 1990s, and despite a creeping sense of marital ennui in some quarters, so it remains. Modern footballers, however, give love a bad name, as a flick through the archives of David Hills' magnificent 'Said & Done' column in the *Observer* will tell you. There are a few players who still have a palpable attachment to their clubs: Lionel Messi at Barcelona, Liverpool's Jamie Carragher, Thierry Henry and Arsenal. But for many, love and loyalty have become little more than bargaining chips (every kiss of the badge ratchets future transfer fees that little bit higher) or prefab excuses (restless Robbie Keane can't help it that he got the call from his boyhood club ~~Liverp~~ ~~Celt~~ ~~West~~ LA Galaxy). In May 2009, Arsenal's Kolo Touré went a big rubbery one at the thought of how much he adored life in north London. 'People know I love the Club, nobody can say I don't,' he declared. 'I believe you can only truly love one club in your career, and my club is Arsenal!' Two months later, after joining Manchester City, he had a variation on the same theme. 'When you love a woman and she gives you back the love, you are really happy, and that's what I can see at City. They have given me the love and I'm really delighted to bring back the love.' Emmanuel Adebayor went for the same kind of line when he left City for Real Madrid on loan: 'When I come to Madrid... I feel that the fans love me... there is nothing more important than to feel loved.' A few months later, the ex-Arsenal striker joined Spurs on loan.

Why the pretence? There's a reason for Benoît Assou-Ekotto's popularity beyond the confines of White Hart Lane, and it's that he doesn't try and kid anybody. He doesn't love Tottenham. He doesn't even love football. He's just good enough at it to make a living, and it's a good one, so that's what he's doing – who cares that you know it? It warms the cockles and various other parts of the anatomy to know a player is as daft about your club as you are, but you can at least respect a man who thinks better than to try and bullshit you.

If you want to know how much a player really loves the club, see if he's puckering up to the badge after you've been relegated. While you dig out your *A-Z* of Barnsley and allow yourself to get mildly excited about seeing what the catering's like at Ashton Gate these days, chances are he's already on the phone to his agent. 'Guys today, noted Tony Soprano,' have no room for the penal experience.' Football's equivalent of a spell in the big house – a season or two in the lower leagues – is something that very few people in English football are willing to countenance. Back in the day established internationals such as Trevor Brooking, Stuart Pearce – the England captain at the time – and Lou Macari were happy to do a season or three in the lower leagues.

There are a few modern examples, most notably Gianluigi Buffon and Alessandro Del Piero, who stayed with Juventus following their *Calciopoli*-related demotion from Serie A in 2006 (Buffon opted to look on the bright side, announcing that he'd never won Serie B and it might be nice to give it a go). But many players turn their noses up at a stint at a lower level – despite the evidence of the relegation season, modern footballers seem to think the second tier is beneath them in more ways than one. Jermain Defoe submitted a transfer request within 24 hours of West Ham's relegation in 2003, although that seemed polite by Pascal Chimbonda's standards. Wigan were not relegated in 2006 but Chimbonda, who had just had a superb first season in English football, decided it was time to move on. Never mind the fact that Wigan had rescued his floundering career. As soon as the last game of the season, a 4–2 defeat at Arsenal, had finished, Chimbonda pulled a transfer request out of his sock and handed it to the manager, Paul Jewell. The contents of a footballer's sock are usually pretty pungent after a match, but this was on a whole new level.

EVERYONE'S AT IT

You should never judge a football match by the headlines. When we think of England's World Cup semi-final defeat to West Germany in 1990, we generally focus on two things: the lottery of penalties, and the dramatic rollover from Thomas Berthold that got Paul Gascoigne booked for a second time – so excluding him from the final had England won – and prompted the tears of England's clown prince.

It was probably a fair decision, but one that left a slightly bitter taste because of the reaction of Berthold: felled by the tackle, he rolled about like a cheese down a Gloucestershire hill, ensuring that Gascoigne was booked. The West German bench also leapt to the sideline to demonstrate their displeasure at the tackle. Perhaps neither influenced the referee, the generally excellent Brazilian José Roberto Wright, but he was certainly under pressure to show the yellow card he pulled from his pocket.

It's easy to conclude from this incident, taken in isolation, that England were done by German gamesmanship, and to assume the whole game followed a similar pattern. Berthold's overreaction, however, is a totally unfair reflection of what was, in fact, one of the noblest games of modern times. When Chris Waddle missed the decisive penalty, Lothar Matthäus eschewed the obvious desire to celebrate, instead going straight to Waddle to comfort him. Throughout the game, players helped opponents to their feet after almost every challenge. When Gascoigne was booted up in the air from behind by Andreas Brehme, a simply appalling challenge, a couple of moments after being booked, we feared he would turn round and land one on Brehme. Instead he calmly shook his hand and got on with business.

This match was exceptional even by the standards of the day – in the *Guardian* two days later, David Lacey commented that 'Wednesday's game set welcome standards of sportsmanship' – but not by much. Back then, it was normal for 22 men, men being the operative word, to go up against each other in a battle of skill and will, everyone sharing one simple attitude: may the best team win. Everyone wanted to win, of course, but it was just as important that they won in a certain way. Watch any of the old matches on ESPN Classic and you will see a similar thing. Sportsmanship was a simple norm, consistently manifesting itself in generosity of spirit. In the 1968 European Cup final, when Alex Stepney stopped the great Eusébio scoring a late winner for Benfica against Manchester United, Eusébio's first reaction was to shake Stepney's hand in congratulation. The iconic photograph of Pelé and Bobby Moore after Brazil's victory over England in 1970, in which the two men shake hands after swapping shirts, is a perfect encapsulation of the respect that was generally in evidence.

That is no longer the case. In the 21st century there is no such respect; as the sense of entitlement that leads to such charmless behaviour off the pitch encroaches on to the field of play, footballers are often all too happy to win matches by foul means or fouler. Old footballers were not always the prettiest or most elegant of players, but at least they weren't sneaky about it. Modern footballers, on the other hand, give the impression they would be only too happy to stab you in the back. Then blame someone else. Then fall over clutching their face. It's amusing that football is still regularly described as 'a man's game' when every other week some of the biggest talking points revolve around grown men behaving in a manner that would shame the most petulant of bairns. Not even the biggest events – the 2010 World Cup final, the 2011 Champions League semi-final between Barcelona and Real Madrid – remain untainted. Barça's first-leg trip to the Bernabéu was breathlessly anticipated and Lionel Messi's second goal was immaculate, but the match immediately became known as the Game of Shame thanks to an almost constant stream of sly fouls and brawling on the sidelines. At least 698,834,593 of the 700 million people who watched the World Cup final between Holland and Spain a year earlier, in which there were 14 yellow cards and at least eight players could legitimately have been sent off (although only Holland's John Heitinga was, after picking up two bookings), complained of being put off their dinner by the brutal 120-minute ravaging of about every last Corinthian ideal.[4]

By that point, of course, we'd witnessed Sergio Busquets's peekaboo antics during Barcelona's 2010 Champions League semi-final meeting with Internazionale. When Thiago Motta, shielding the ball, gave Busquets a hand-off to the neck, Busquets immediately went down like he had been kneecapped by some of Edinburgh's finest. While rolling around on the floor, with both hands to his face, Busquets peeked through his hands to see what action the referee was taking. It was the sort of nonsense that compromises the legacy of one of the most beautiful sides in football history and that flagrantly contravenes the ideals of the game itself, yet the game's governing bodies remain reluctant to act retrospectively. No wonder, then, that David Navarro was so shameless when he travelled to Athletic Bilbao with Valencia. Having split his opponent's head open with his elbow, Navarro dropped to the floor with deathly relaxed muscles and stayed there, not moving. Still playing dead, he was stretchered off as the referee, who hadn't seen the collision properly, hushed the vociferously complaining Bilbao players. 'And then he got up, and ran onto the pitch, everything entirely intact,' wrote Sid Lowe, for *Sports Illustrated*. 'Except

---

[4] Holland were involved in an equally notorious match at the previous World Cup, in 2006, against Portugal, yet what the *Guardian*'s report described as 'an evening of mayhem and spite' was, for many viewers, something of a guilty pleasure. The difference centres on the honesty of each game: in 2006, everyone lost their heads completely, and there are few things funnier than watching a grown man who has completely lost his rag. In contrast, the melodramatics of 2010 and 2011 bore the sorry hallmarks of cynical, pre-planned tactics.

his credibility.' It says something that men who used to laugh until they gasped for air at the women's game watched the 2011 women's World Cup and instead choked on the sight of players riding tackles, accepting refereeing decisions, and generally getting on with the game, despite the fact that all the excuses for dishonesty that we're increasingly forced to swallow – the silverware, the prestige, the pressure – might have been served up.

'The game has to change, we have reached a point where diving is almost becoming a tolerated part of the game. But it is cheating. Fans hate diving and the Football Association should give a three-game ban to anyone who is caught diving.' Forgive us for citing rent-a-quote ex-referee Jeff Winter (this time he was endorsing a newly developed set of anti-diving shin pads) but he's got a point. Where once we were treated to innovations like the Cruyff turn, or the Zidane spin, now we're treated to the Busquets tumble and the Drogba dive. We've become so accustomed to seeing players exaggerate collisions that when Didier Drogba was accidentally knocked out cold by Norwich City goalkeeper John Ruddy in August 2011, ITV commentator Clive Tyldesley remarked on Twitter: 'Glad I wasn't commentating when Drogba copped a nasty one. Not sure how sympathetic I'd have been initially.' Tyldesley went on to wish the Chelsea striker well, but it's long since stopped being easy to be so generous. After a Francis Jeffers dive against Liverpool in 2002, Peter Osgood said he was 'the biggest cheat in football' and that he would 'love to see him get really hurt'.

Winter was the referee that day, and awarded Jeffers the penalty, helping Arsenal to level the game, but we're all pretty much agreed on two points. First, diving goes against everything fans want and expect from the game, and second, that it is cheating, plain and simple. Law 12: 'A player must be cautioned for unsporting behaviour, e.g. if a player… attempts to deceive the referee by feigning injury or pretending to have been fouled [and/or] acts in a manner which shows a lack of respect for the game.' None of this nonsense about *making sure the referee knows there was contact*, or *drawing the foul*, or even *everyone does it* – anyone who really believes that diving is fair on the basis that every player has the same opportunity to do it wants locking in a room with a copy of *Tom Brown's Schooldays*. It's just not cricket. The former president of the International Association for the Philosophy of Sport, Dr Cesar R. Torres, has a high-falutin' theory on how bad a fit diving is with the skills that football demands, and how ill-judged justifications – essentially two wrongs make a right – are, but he said it best in a piece for the *New York Times* in 2009: 'Divers fail to honour the game's excellence, that they are supposed to cultivate and celebrate.'

After Argentina striker Ariel Ortega's dive-and-head butt double-whammy at the 1998 World Cup, FIFA suit Keith Cooper warned that football was experiencing 'a little bit of a [diving] epidemic… once it starts, it spreads like wildfire.' As with a number of football's ills, of course, diving is not new, it has simply become more prevalent. Francis Lee was having problems staying upright back in the late sixties; in 1971/72, he scored a record 15 penalties, many of them after he had been cynically taken out by fresh air. In one game for Manchester City, he accused George Best of diving with a crowd-pleasing belly flop – as shameless an example of the pot disparaging the kettle's colour as you are likely to find. And in fact, Best scarcely, if ever, dived. His greatest strength was his astonishing balance, which allowed him to survive the most vicious challenges from the phalanx of hatchet men who populated English football in the late sixties and early seventies. One of Best's more famous goals came in such circumstances, in a League Cup tie in 1970/71. The *Guardian*'s Scott Murray called it 'one of football's greatest-ever juxtapositions of beauty and the beast': Best was running through on goal when, just outside the box, Chelsea's infamous beast Ron 'Chopper' Harris hit him with a brutal, full-speed reducer from behind. Best's body was contorted savagely, with the top half of his body at a 60-degree angle, but he stayed on his feet, slipped round the goalkeeper and passed the ball into the net. Then, only then, did he go down, bowing to the adoring Stretford End. It was impossibly poetic.

Another legendary example of a player attempting to stay on his feet came in the opening match of Italia 90, when Argentina's Claudio Caniggia was the subject of a brutal three-stage hit from Cameroon. He rode the first challenge, staggered through the second, and was just about retaining his balance, eyes only for the ball, when Benjamin Massing ended all doubts with an absurd hit from the side. With the likely exception of Lionel Messi, most modern footballers would have gone over after the first tackle. Some 21 years after Diego Maradona slalomed his way through the England team and around Peter Shilton at Mexico 86, Messi, who hadn't even been born at the time, scored an almost identical goal for Barcelona against Getafe. The similarity was close enough that Catalan television played a split-screen video of the two strikes and created an instant YouTube hit, appreciated as much for its retro charm as its aesthetic value. As a general rule, we've stopped expecting players to stay up unless they're actually brought down.

Nowadays, 'contact' has become synonymous with 'foul', and if a player detects or even anticipates the slightest of touches from his opponent, he is 'entitled to go down'. Entitled to go down? Just because it isn't quite a fresh-air dive, it doesn't mean the spirit of the game isn't getting clobbered; the second the slightest whiff of the idea of such entitlement hits the back of the throat it should caress the gag reflex into sustained *Exorcist*-style projectile vomiting. Instead, 'entitled to go down' has become part of football's lexicon without so much as a wet hiccup. Players have actually developed a pathetic habit of dragging their leg into a defender's, yet nine times out of ten it passes without comment. Those who opt not to take up the chance to roll around on the floor are disparaged, even by managers who'd never baldly promote *diving*. 'It's a nailed-on penalty but he tried to stay up, he was too honest,' said the Tottenham manager Harry Redknapp, after Robbie Keane's failure to fall over when tackled by Chelsea's Ricardo Carvalho, at 1–0 down, at the start of the 2009/10 season. The Gillingham manager Andy Hessenthaler said much the same in February 2011, when striker Cody McDonald stayed on his feet under pressure – and shot wide – rather than dropping to the floor. 'He could have thought about maybe going down, but that's the honesty of the lad. A more proven striker may have been cleverer and gone down. I don't like to see it, but it happens, and the clever ones would have got a penalty.'

Too honest? Not very clever? It's like hearing judges mocking petty thieves for not having the cojones to walk into a bank with a sawn-off shotgun under their arms. On the flip side, commentators will offer players who respond to a tough tackle by picking themselves up and dusting themselves down (it happens, occasionally) a congratulatory pat on the back – a 'Well done, lad', just for *not* pretending to be injured.

How did these corrupt value judgments come to be so commonplace – so banal – in a game like football?

Reprising Black Grape's Euro 96 single 'England's Irie' (one version of which begins: 'Internationale psyche / you dive, we no likey'), plenty of people still argue that it's all down to Johnny Foreigner. In 2009, then England captain John Terry reckoned it wasn't just individuals, but that all English players were 'too honest' to dive, and that it was costing them in European and international competitions. Though he berated Jeffers for diving, Peter Osgood placed the blame elsewhere, saying, 'Since the foreigners came over here, everyone's at it. Even the English lads.' Similarly, Terry's vice-captain Steven Gerrard wrote in his autobiography that 'players like [Cristiano] Ronaldo and [Ricardo] Carvalho are damaging football'. Yet his own gravitational issues are archived for posterity on YouTube – and his book, published in 2006, came less than six months after a particularly amusing fresh-air crumple against Bolton. Who knows for how many league games Arsenal's Invincibles would have gone unbeaten but for Wayne Rooney's fall at Old Trafford in 2004? His cynical opportunism as Sol Campbell stupidly but harmlessly wafted a foot into his path arguably changed the course of English football history. Most of England's top players have dived, even if, in the finest English tradition, they're often more ham-fisted than their continental counterparts – Theo Walcott felt moved to issue a public apology after failing to sell a dive to the referee's assistant as Arsenal threatened to lose to Leeds in an FA Cup tie in early 2011. ('Fair play to Theo for apologising!' Tweeted his teammate, Jack Wilshere, afterwards, before unleashing an unconvincing dose of *virtus*: 'Takes a real man to apologise!')

It shouldn't really surprise us to find owning up to cheating taken as some sort of emblem of sportsmanship, because genuine instances are becoming increasingly rare in this crooked age of phantom rights and vanished morality. In 1988, when Werder Bremen defender Frank Ordenewitz informed the referee, who'd just awarded a corner to Cologne, that he'd actually handled the ball and therefore conceded a penalty, it was uncommon but not considered extraordinary – or stupid. Paolo Di Canio was awarded the FIFA Fair Play Award in 2001 for stopping play instead of shooting into an empty net when the Everton keeper Paul Gerrard went down lame. In 1997 Robbie Fowler was also praised by FIFA for asking the referee Gerald Ashby not to give a penalty against Arsenal after he'd leapt over David Seaman's challenge. Yet the reaction to Fowler – for every two people hailing a rare act of sportsmanship, there was one suggesting that Fowler had behaved disingenuously – showed that modern sport is no place for a Good Samaritan.

We don't mean to pick on Theo Walcott, but, well, at this point, we're going to, because when Andrei Arshavin tried to stop the referee awarding a penalty with Arsenal 1–0 up against Portsmouth in May 2009, Walcott practically boasted about intervening. 'I saw Andrei doing it and I ran over to him, because if you're 1–0 up away from home and the referee's given a penalty, you don't want to tell him it's not one,' he said, as if he'd stopped a small child from pulling a hot pan off the hob. 'It just showed what an honest guy he is, but when you're going for the win you need to do the dirty things.' (Walcott was in a cleaner mood, however, when told that someone from Portsmouth spat in his drink during the game: 'That's just not appropriate in this sport.')

He's not the only one trying to get a foothold on the moral

high ground, by any means – not a game goes by in which at least one player doesn't wave an imaginary card at the referee. A frightening number of modern footballers seem able to fraudulently summon the anger of the wronged even when they are palpably in the wrong – how often do we see players appeal for a throw-in or a corner even though theirs was clearly the last touch? Players are generally happy to toe the line that none of them is bigger than the club, yet they often appear to think they're above the law, drawn to the sound of a referee's whistle like flies around a horse's backside. It's not that we want to pick on John Terry, you understand, but again, we're going to. As Chelsea captain, Terry has the right to discuss decisions with the referee, but in September 2007 he decided the armband also gave him licence to try and snatch the red card shown to John Obi Mikel out of Mike Dean's hand. There are infants with a better sense of decorum and responsibility. The ways in which players attempt to manipulate the referee are both embarrassing and depressing, especially when you contrast them with other sports: in rugby, it is commonplace to see an 18-stone beast of a man nodding meekly at a pint-sized referee. Which is just as it should be.

HARDER, BETTER, FASTER, STRONGER

Of the many ways a fan could relate to a player in the past, few were greater than the sight of a man wheezing after his own first touch, his gut pressing insistently at the tight polyester of his shirt. Though we know that the increased professionalism of football is largely a positive development, we reserve the right to add it to the list of worthy things – a meat-free diet, reusable nappies, *The One Show* – whose reality we don't completely and utterly relish. It's absurd, chanting 'you fat bastard' at men with six-packs. Where are the portly players of old? No one's been eating all the pies!

For almost all of his lustrous career, Ronaldo was able to carry a bit of extra weight and still excel at the very highest level, and a bit of flab was no problem for short, stocky geniuses like Diego Maradona and Romário. Indeed Romário insisted he played better if he'd downed calories aplenty the night before. Ferenc Puskás, whom many regard as the greatest player of all time, simply loved eating. After his Honvéd side visited Molineux in 1954, the Wolves captain Billy Wright watched him scoff at least 12 crackers with butter and cheese. It didn't do him too much harm. A generous waistline has always leant a bit of extra colour to the game. William Foulke, who kept goal for Sheffield United and Chelsea at the turn of the 20th century, is still the heaviest first-class footballer on record, weighing 22 stone even in his prime. During his one appearance for England, he snapped the crossbar in half, and when during a league game he accidentally landed on top of Sheffield Wednesday's Laurie Bell, he thought he'd killed him. Yet he was considered unbeatable for much of his career, helping United to the First Division title in 1898. 'The manner in which he gets down to low shots explodes any idea that a superfluity of flesh is a handicap,' according to one write-up.

Foulke is an extreme from another time, but it is only recently that the fat footballer has become an endangered species. Christened 'Fatty Arbuckle' by Crystal Palace chairman Simon Jordan, Neil Ruddock once calculated that he had eaten 212 steak and kidney pies in a year. In 2001/02, Swindon had to commission a pair of shorts for him after he had failed to fit into all 86 pairs that the club had; Ruddock was a disgrace to professionalism, but you have to admire his not inconsiderable front. According to Stan Collymore, Ruddock once sat eating a bacon sandwich in the Liverpool gym until warned that the assistant manager Ronnie Moran was approaching, at which point he dumped the evidence in his training bag, poured water over his head to simulate sweat, and started panting on the treadmill. Moran pointed to Ruddock as an example of the commitment needed to reach the top.

The stories in football's Old Testament had a bit of meat on them, and often the distinct whiff of fermented hops. During his time playing under Brian Clough at Nottingham Forest, Teddy Sheringham grabbed one of the glasses of half-time orange juice that were on a tray in the dressing room. 'I took a long swig and for the next ten seconds I couldn't breathe,' he said. 'It was a very large, barely diluted, vodka and orange.' It could belong to only one man. Clough locked the team in a hotel room before the 1979 League Cup final, insisting they get through two huge crates before being released; half the side went to bed hammered, but they beat Southampton the next day. Earlier that season, Clough sensed an unusual nervousness on the way to Anfield for the second leg of a European Cup tie. He stopped off at a pub, made each player drink a couple, and later that day they easily secured the 0–0 draw they needed to put the holders Liverpool out of the cup on aggregate.

Alcohol has played its part in the decline of one or two of English football's finest players, and Clough's last years in football make for a powerful case against it, but booze has often been a vital tool in building team spirit. In the world of cricket, Australian batsman David Boon downed a record 52 cans of lager on the flight to London for the 1989 Ashes series, went to a cocktail party after landing and then slept for 36 hours. Yet he made more catches than anyone else (nine) and averaged 55 runs an innings as Australia claimed the Ashes with a 4–0 whitewash. 'You played for each other, for the team, for the moment in the dressing room,' said opening batsman Geoff Marsh. 'That's the thing everyone loved doing – getting in that dressing room after a good day and having a couple of drinks and a laugh.' Examining alcohol's fraternal qualities, social psychologists coined the phrase 'liquid bonding'. Most of English football's great teams just before and just after the start of the Premier League were notorious for their booze culture, from Arsenal's Tuesday Club to Sir Alex Ferguson's first great Manchester United side.

There is a salient point here, among the anecdotes. Clough revelled in the fact that John Robertson, the X-factor in his European Cup-winning sides, was fat. Before Forest's second final, against Cologne in 1980, the subject of Cologne's experienced international right-back Manny Kaltz came up in an interview. 'We've got a fat little man who will destroy him,' said Clough gleefully. Robertson scored the only goal of the game. Clough knew his team had a vanilla hue without Robertson's genius on the wing, and it was often the case that larger players brought something different to the table in more than one sense. They provided the flair of the side. An exclusive focus on athleticism is dangerous, and today's football is often too fast, a helter-skelter ride of witlessness. This trend has been increasing for years, and there was something disconcerting when, in 2006, the England manager Steve McClaren described Micah Richards as a 'new breed of player – strong, quick, athletic and mobile'. Not a single mention of skill. Gareth Bale, the PFA Player of the

Year in 2010/11, is extremely talented, best demonstrated by a technically immaculate left-footed volley against Stoke at the start of that season, but his core strengths are athletic. Watching Bale roast a full-back over a 30-yard sprint is utterly exhilarating, but it doesn't engage the soul in the way that someone like Robertson did.

One of the other charming things about Robertson's Forest team was its rumpled, not-so-much-as-a-brush appearance, Ian Bowyer's shock of ginger hair as untamed as Kenny Burns's top lip. Professionalism has given us a game of raw power played by men with manicures. 'I use skin creams, perfumes and conditioners, and I will shave every hair off my body,' said Lazio's Mauro Zárate ahead of his wedding in March 2011. 'I will look fantastic.' We miss the ugly men of old, the ones whose features could only belong to a footballer, whether it's a nose that has been broken in 14 different places, an eye the size of a small village or a vacant row of front teeth. A footballer should look like he has done a proper day's – well, 90 minutes' – work. Just as a miner isn't going to come home smelling of lavender and musk, a footballer should not be in a position to strut down either the catwalk or the wing.

Joe Jordan, the Scottish forward who scored at the 1974, 1978 and 1982 World Cups, knew that a ball in the net was worth three front teeth splattered in the six-yard box, having been booted out by a defender. Jordan lost so many front teeth that he ended up using dentures that he would take out before each match. Ostensibly this was for safety reasons, but the fact it made him look like an even more terrifying version of Jaws from James Bond's *The Spy Who Loved Me* was a happy by-product. Nowadays players are much more reluctant to put their head among flying boots. Indeed the facial imperfections were endearingly position-specific. Goalkeepers and defenders generally had to watch the nose, forwards the teeth, and midfielders the lot. Steve Ogrizovic and Steve Bruce, goalkeeper and defender at Coventry City and Manchester United respectively, both had noses shaped like modern-art monstrosities. Even the elegant Willie Maddren, the Middlesbrough central defender whom the great Hugh McIlvanney described as England's best uncapped player, broke his nose on his first-team debut. This was the footballer's rite of passage, the polyester-collar worker's badge of honour.

After the 1959 FA Cup final, Nottingham Forest's man of the match, Stewart Imlach, completely forgot to grab his false teeth from the dugout (where the manager Billy Walker had stashed the team's collection in a hanky) and had to flash the Queen a gappy smile as he collected his winner's medal. Right at the outset of *My Father and Other Working-Class Football Heroes,* a kind of archaeological dig for the artefacts of his father's career, Gary Imlach observes the critical difference between then and now: 'My father and his teammates came from the same stock as those who packed the terraces every week to watch them. And they knew they were heading back into that community when their playing days were over – perhaps more accurately, had never really left.'

CHAPTER 2

THE MISERABLE GAME

W inning is for losers. Many of life's more interesting stories focus on those who didn't quite make it; who didn't get the girl or the job or the epiphany or even the Jules Rimet trophy. Johan Cruyff said his Holland side of the 70s were immortalised by the fact they did *not* win the World Cup and, when *World Soccer* magazine invited a group of experts to select the greatest teams of all time in 2007, three of the top seven sides won nothing: Hungary 1953, Holland 1974 and Brazil 1982.

Sport is about – or at least should be about – more than victory. It should be about derring-do and heroism, about performing with a style that transcends the tedious focus on results. A winner's medal is not necessary for a place in the pantheon. This is true in any sport; just ask the likes of Jimmy White – six-time runner-up in snooker's World Championship final, yet often referred to as 'The People's

Champion' — or the enduringly popular Greg Norman, who finished second seven times in golf's Major championships (though he did win The Open on two occasions). Or, more recently, Judd Trump, who charmed snooker fans and non-snooker fans alike with a swaggering performance in the 2011 World Championship. They and others like them lost finals, but so what? They thrilled the fans with their play and at the end of the match they wore a huge smile, because they knew they had earned something much rarer and more precious than victory: glory, and in industrial quantities.

This is not to say winning is incidental; far from it. The peculiar modern desire to simplify almost everything in football into the richest black and white means that you are supposed to fall strictly into one of two camps, defined by two equally famous quotes. 'The most important thing is not winning but taking part', from Baron Pierre de Coubertin, the founder of the modern Olympic Games; and 'Winning isn't everything, it's the only thing', from the ultra-quotable American football coach, Henry Russell 'Red' Sanders.

As Michael Douglas says in *Wonder Boys*, it's a little more *complicated* than that.

THE PRICE OF VICTORY

Opinions on the importance of victory are almost as unique as snowflakes, and it is palpably possible to be both a serial winner and an incurable romantic. Take, for example, Bill Shankly, winner of three league titles, two FA Cups and one UEFA Cup while manager at Liverpool, and credited with turning the club into one of football's major forces. 'If you are first you are first,' he famously said, 'if you are second you are nothing.' Yet he knew that there was a way to finish first. 'He did not fit everybody's idea of a romantic,' wrote Hugh McIlvanney of Shankly after his death in 1981. 'But that's what he was, an out-and-out, 22-carat example of the species. His secret was that he sensed deep down that the only practical approach to sport is the romantic one.'

Glory, not victory, is the soul of football. Nobody made that point better than Bill Nicholson, manager of Tottenham Hotspur through their heyday from the late 1950s to the early 1970s: 'It is better to fail aiming high than to succeed aiming low. And we of Spurs have set our sights very high, so high in fact that even failure will have in it an echo of glory.' Danny Blanchflower (the brilliant captain of Nicholson's Double-winning side of 1960/61) brought that philosophy to the field of play: 'The great fallacy is that the game is first and last about winning,' he said. 'It's nothing of the kind. The game is about glory. It is about doing things in style, with a flourish, about going out to beat the other lot, not waiting for them to die of boredom.'

Nicholson and Blanchflower were old souls, and modern football is no country for those. For the most part, winning is all that matters these days. We have seen the lengths to which players will go to achieve victory, and it is no different for managers. They may not dive to win a penalty or get an opponent sent off – in fact, though there was little that was dignified about their set-to during a Wednesday night kick-off in 2010, it was noticeable that Everton manager David Moyes took a proper shove from his Manchester City counterpart Roberto Mancini rather more robustly than, say, Joey Barton did when slapped by Arsenal forward Gervinho in August 2011 – but they have shown willing in other ways. (As the countless FA hearings and touchline bans in recent times attest, pre-emptive criticism of referees has been a particular favourite.)

The most persuasive imperatives are written in numbers. 'THE £90 MILLION GAME'. That was what the 2010 Championship play-off final between Blackpool and Cardiff was dubbed. Victory would bring promotion to the Premier League and a cash windfall like no other. The financial incentives for achievement – whether it is winning a competition, qualifying for the Champions League or avoiding relegation – are so much greater than they were in previous decades. In 1986 the 92 clubs of the Football League signed a two-year television rights deal worth £6.3 million; in 2009, the 20 clubs of the Premier League agreed broadcast deals worth £1.782 billion. Wallets duly fattened, the importance of avoiding relegation from the top flight has never been greater. After Newcastle United went down at the end of the 2008/09 season, their accounts showed an immediate drop in revenue of £17.1 million; within two years the deficit for a relegated club was estimated to be £25 million. These kinds of figures have, as Chapter Four explores further, caused most chairmen to develop twitchy trigger fingers. Managers, desperate to avoid the sack, will do whatever it takes to get results.

There is often more to it than the desire to save their own skin: in 2005, the then manager of Bolton Wanderers, Sam Allardyce, highlighted a more human side. 'This club has about 250 employees, maybe more if you count the staff at the hotel that is built into the stadium, and at least half of them would be made redundant if we were relegated,' said Allardyce. 'I am in charge of results at this club, so I have a massive responsibility to all of those people to make sure that Bolton stay in the Premiership. Results are the first priority and then entertainment, so I'd like to know what others would do in my position if they had the responsibility that lies on my shoulders. Devastation lies in relegation and I have to think about what would happen to the young staff with families if we lost our Premiership status.'

Some will react cynically to such a justification for results-orientated football, but it is demonstrably the case that the leading football clubs have become gargantuan entities in the Premier League era; even a relatively small club like Portsmouth had to shed close to 100 jobs when relegated and placed into administration in 2010. Though clubs do not always bear the burden of responsibility very... responsibly, they can usually be relied upon to demonstrate an acute sense of their own importance. And as many a football fan will wearily attest, this kind of self-importance inevitably leads to a sort of never-ending self-validation that places unjustified emphasis on results. A multi-million dollar business, football has been reduced to a transaction despite our own sense that it shouldn't be. We might even ascribe this tendency to a society growing ever more reluctant to make value judgments, happy instead to compliment the Emperor on his fine threads. Manchester United were only very good in fits and starts as they won the 2010/11 Premier League trophy, yet the idea flourished that the title might actually be more laudable for having been won 'badly'.

ALL DEFENCE AND NO GOALS MAKE FOOTBALL A DULL GAME

This chapter opened with *World Soccer*'s selection of the greatest teams, three of whom had won nothing but four of whom amply decorated their trophy cabinets. The Real Madrid side of 1956–60 won five consecutive European Cups, as well as a couple of league titles; the AC Milan team that won back-to-back European cups in 1989 and 1990; and two Brazil sides – the 1958 XI and the 1970 team that featured the likes of Pelé (he had made his World Cup debut as a 17-year-old 12 years earlier), Jairzinho, Rivelino and Tostão amongst others – both won World Cups. Indeed, the 1970 team not only won all six of their qualifying games, but also all six of their tournament games on their way to the Jules Rimet trophy. Yet when it comes to winning matches, the modern football manager has increasingly eschewed the spirit that epitomised such teams.

On Sunday May 22nd 1983, the Football League president Jack Dunnett explained on TV's *Face the Press* that he only ever wanted to see his team (Notts County) win, and he didn't really care how they did it – adding that he could watch Brazil if he wanted to see something special. A day earlier, Brighton and Hove Albion had drawn 2–2 with Manchester United in the FA Cup final, pushing it to a replay for the third year in a row after 60 years in which only one final had required a second go. There was ample opportunity to bemoan the apparently creeping inability to win outright within 90 or even 120 minutes, but such was the quality of the first encounter – 'An epic tale that bears repeating,' ran the *Guardian* headline – that the replay was actually much looked forward to. And, though Brighton were soundly beaten 4–0 at the second attempt, the *Observer*'s Hugh McIlvanney took the opportunity to mock Dunnett's attitude, and his presumption that he spoke for the sensible majority. 'The League might spread their President's wisdom to the previously neutral millions up and down the country whose affections were taken prisoner by Brighton's challenge for the FA Cup,' he wrote, pressing his tongue into his cheek, 'and who refused to be desolated by Thursday evening's events at Wembley.' He even quoted Blanchflower.

Contrast that to United's 2007 FA Cup final meeting with Chelsea, which finished 0–0 before being decided in Chelsea's favour by Didier Drogba's extra-time strike. Even the BBC, which had gone to greater lengths than usual in its coverage of the first FA Cup final at the new Wembley, admitted the match was 'unlikely to live long in the memory', and it was dubbed on the 606 forum the 'Most Boring Cup Final in History'. Managers have carefully lobotomised glory from their definition of victory, and the result is boring, defensive football. In the 21st century, football is arguably as defensive as it has ever been; while a strong case could also be made for the sides of the late 80s and the mid 90s, modern teams demonstrate not just evolution from their proto-cagey predecessors, but also a *revolution* in terms of the ultimate aim of the man at the helm. Once it was to score one more goal than the opposition; now the manager's plan is to concede one fewer. Defence has become not just a priority, but *the* priority. That philosophical switch is the essence of how football has changed in recent times. (The chorus to the unofficial England 1998 World Cup song, Fat Les's 'Vindaloo', included the words: 'We're gonna score one more than you, ENGLAND!' If they redo it in future, they will do well to make 'We're gonna concede one fewer than you, ENGLAND!' scan just as effectively.)

That managers consistently prioritise defence at the expense of their side's attacking options has an undeniable logic to it, destruction being intrinsically easier to control than creation. For the fans, however, it has made for an increasingly unstimulating spectacle; there cannot have been many duller years in football than 2004, when Rafael Benítez won the UEFA Cup (with Valencia), José Mourinho won the Champions League (with Porto) and Greece, a chronically limited side playing stultifying football under Otto Rehhagel, won Euro 2004. Johann Cruyff espoused a deliberately simple game-plan: 'if you score one more than your opponent, you win.' In 2006, when Rio Ferdinand scored an injury-time winner for Manchester United against Liverpool, the then United assistant manager Carlos Queiroz proudly boasted his own straightforward strategy: 'Our aim was to score *one* goal.' During the 2010 World Cup, Queiroz – undoubtedly a brilliant defensive coach – was in charge of Portugal, a side boasting in their ranks Cristiano Ronaldo, fresh from scoring 33 goals in his debut season at Real Madrid, yet they scored in just one of their four games. (Yes, yes, they put seven past North Korea, but is that a team you really want to hang your argument on? They've started two World Cup final tournaments and shipped 21 goals.) Queiroz's über-defensive approach leaked just a single goal in those four games, yet such was the focus on blocking out their opponents that the team floundered even when it had the opportunity to attack, making an ignominious second-round exit after losing 1–0 to Spain.

Queiroz is a fine example of the perils of overly defensive football, but another Portuguese coach, José Mourinho, is the high priest of this new negativity – a fact even those of us who are hopelessly seduced by his unique brand of charisma, contempt and certainty, not to mention the Tyler Durden-esque devotion he inspires in his players, would struggle to deny.

The difference between Queiroz and Mourinho is that while the former is naturally defensively minded, the latter has the ability and, occasionally, the will to inspire quite breathtaking attacking football. At times, Mourinho's sides have been wildly entertaining: in his first winter at Chelsea, Damien Duff and Arjen Robben ran riot on the wings and 29 goals were scored in an eight-game spell; in his first season at Real Madrid, Mourinho's side racked up 102 goals in 38 league games, becoming only the third side in Spanish history to reach three figures. (The other two, incidentally, were bossed by British managers: John Toshack with Real Madrid in 1989/90 and Bobby Robson at Barcelona in 1996/97.) After Tottenham Hotspur, who had won only four points at Stamford Bridge in the Premier League era, earned a fifth with a goalless draw in September 2004, Mourinho complained bitterly about the visitors' defensive play. 'Tottenham might as well have put the team bus in front of their goal,' he said. 'We wanted to play, they didn't. We wanted to score, they didn't. Every time they just kicked the ball away. It was frustrating for me, my players, for every Chelsea supporter and for every football supporter.' It wasn't long, however, before this unforgiving appraisal started to look like sanctimony. For the most part, and particularly in the stratospheric games, Mourinho has not so much favoured pragmatism over idealism as booted idealism out of the door and got an injunction against it coming within two miles of the ground.

It's an effective approach, if nothing else, and in the future we will look back and marvel at how he was able to occasionally beat a Barcelona side that swept all others before it, but it can be terrible to watch. 'Madrid are a side with no personality,' said Alfredo Di Stéfano, Real's legendary

Argentine forward of the 1950s and 60s, after watching the team play a dense, defensive game against Barcelona in the Champions League semi-final of 2010/11. 'They just run back and forth constantly, tiring themselves out. Their approach was not right. Barcelona were a lion, Madrid a mouse.' (On this occasion Mourinho's tactics failed to produce victory as Barcelona overcame them with an aggregate score of 3–1 after a two-legged semi-final.)

'The moment of victory is much too short to live for that and nothing else'– so said tennis legend Martina Navratilova, who can't often find herself name-checked in conversations about football, but she makes a point that few managers seem to want to grasp these days. It was Mourinho who was in charge of Chelsea when they won that diabolical FA Cup final in 2007, and afterwards he said of their success: 'I asked the players, "Do you want to enjoy the game, or do you want to enjoy after the game?" The players told me they wanted to enjoy after the game so I said: "OK, then we will enjoy after the game."' When Alan Smith, the former Arsenal striker who now works for Sky Sports and the *Daily Telegraph*, wrote about Mourinho's quote, he said: 'All this took me back to my time at Arsenal, where George Graham's words stand out to this day. "You might not always enjoy playing for me," he once said in an address to the squad (he was right). "But if we've been successful you'll look back on our time together with great pride and affection."'

This is all well and good if you only care how much the cleaner hates the job of keeping the trophy cabinet clean, but it doesn't show much concern for when the fans might start to be able to enjoy things. It is not for nothing that during Graham's tenure the opposing terraces chanted 'Boring, boring Arsenal'. Of course, if we could have our cake and eat it – watch our team play glorious football *and* win – then surely we would. No one wants to play gloriously and lose eternally, but it's never been a case of either/or: there isn't a single example of a club playing exciting, attacking football and losing every match they ever played. On their return to the top flight in 2010/11, Blackpool came within a whisker of staying up having opted not to abandon the attacking football that had seen them promoted in the first place, at a time when we'd become accustomed to the Premier League's newcomers defending for their lives and expiring in any case. If you're going to fall on your sword, at least make sure you're dying happy.

This is not to pick on Chelsea or Arsenal, Mourinho or Graham, because such a position is widespread; it's just that in most cases it is unspoken. Instead it is a pervading attitude that threatens little by little to suffocate the spirit of the game. This relentlessly pragmatic approach is hardly the fantasy of small children, running round the local park, wanting to be Pelé or Maradona or Messi. Former Scotland international Steve Archibald's famous quote, that 'team spirit is an illusion glimpsed in the aftermath of victory', is both brilliant and flexible. We could say with equal conviction that an enjoyment of football is an illusion glimpsed in the aftermath of victory.

Nothing illustrates better the tendency for fans to rewrite their emotions than any one of the Champions League semi-final meetings between Mourinho's Chelsea and the Liverpool side of Spanish manager, Rafael Benítez. Benítez is another modern coach who believes in victory over everything else, his intractable caution leading the media to dub him a 'control freak'. It was the gross misfortune of the neutral fan that Chelsea met Benítez's Liverpool in every

Champions League season during Mourinho's tenure. In direct contravention of basic mathematics, the meeting of two negatives did not make a positive: those six matches between Mourinho and Benítez produced a mere three goals. Overall, in 16 meetings between the two managers, there was a miserly average of 1.69 goals in each.

We're seeing fewer goals various rule changes designed to benefit attackers, including changes to the offside law, the back-pass law, and the clampdown on the tackle from behind. In real terms, the returns have diminished significantly, and it is revealing that since it began, the most common score in the Premier League has been 1–0.

Some people dismiss criticism of a reduction in goals as simplistic, as if it is made by philistines who cannot appreciate a 0–0 draw or football's subtleties. This is, of course, utter nonsense, another example of modern football's need to deal in absolutes. The point, as with so many of football's changes, is of degree. The scarcity of goals is essential for them to matter, and nobody wants to see 7–4 scorelines every week (the result of a record Premier League encounter between Portsmouth and Reading at Fratton Park in 2007). When Arsenal beat Tottenham 5–4 in 2004/05, Mourinho (of course) dismissed it as 'a hockey score'.

As delicious a put-down as that was from Mourinho, one that you can imagine delivered with lordly contempt, Arsène Wenger's approach at Arsenal is eminently preferable to Mourinho's.

There are a few managers who still believe in attack first – Wenger himself, along with the likes of Josep Guardiola and Harry Redknapp. Ian Holloway's resolute adherence to his attacking principles may not have stopped Blackpool being relegated, but they did score a remarkable 55 goals – the highest ever for a relegated team and equal to the number scored by fifth-placed Tottenham. The other two demoted teams, Birmingham City and West Ham United, scored 37 and 43 goals respectively. Wenger, who won two Doubles in his first five years at Arsenal, has shown more flexibility in this regard, switching to the 4-5-1 formation (we're getting to that in a minute) that he had previously bemoaned to get Arsenal to the 2006 Champions League final, but his principles have been more intractable in the last few years. It's alarming that he, and a few others who prioritise attacking football to such a degree, are almost seen as weirdos. Imagine being a romantic! Imagine wanting to entertain! It is extraordinary that during the 2011 Copa America, the 1–1 draw between Uruguay and Chile should stand out as having been a game between 'two sides who wanted to win' (in the words of Luis Suarez), and frankly startling that in his analysis of the tournament for the *Guardian*, Jonathan Wilson should note the rarity of a match that 'showcased two teams with a clear idea of how they go about doing so.'

In stark contrast we have Roberto Mancini (the former manager of Internazionale, a club who, perhaps coincidentally, were subsequently managed by first José Mourinho and then Rafael Benítez). Under his leadership, Manchester City won their first trophy for 35 years when they beat Stoke in the FA Cup final. Yet, whereas Blackpool carried a wage bill of £6 million at the end of the 2009/10 season and a declaration from their president, Valeri Belokon, when they won promotion, that their focus would be on 'determination and belief' rather than a huge outlay on transfers, Manchester City paid out £133 million in wages for the same period. Between their takeover by Sheikh Mansour bin Zayed Al Nahyan in

2008 and the summer that Blackpool won promotion, they spent some £239 million on new players. With such a financial burden, out went any memory of City's last league championship title in 1968, which was secured with a swashbuckling 4–3 win at Newcastle United on the final day of the season. Instead, in came an approach which Mancini himself expressed when he said:'I like 1–0 wins … I prefer we are boring for two to three matches and we win 1–0.'

It was only in August 2011, after hurtling past the half-billion pound mark, that Mancini said that his team needed to 'take more risks', belatedly acknowledging that spending all that money – some of it, even before the summer of 2011, on players capable of startling creativity – and playing boring football wasn't likely to tease the finest adjectives out of City's chroniclers, no matter how many trophies followed. Flick through the pages of any football history and you'll find that aesthetics have always mattered; football is littered with examples of teams who put glory first, daylight second and victory third. It's telling that, in Denmark, the magnificent, free-flowing side who reached the semi-finals of Euro 84 and the second round of Mexico 86 are remembered much more fondly than the cautious team that won Euro 92.

In England, neutrals still get a warm glow when they think of the Oldham side of 1989/90. They reached the semi-final of the FA Cup, the final of the League Cup, and missed out on promotion to the First Division by a mere three points. The same is true of the Italian side Foggia in 1991/92. When they were promoted to Serie A for the first time in 25 years, their coach Zdeněk Zeman looked at the usual way of doing things and decided, sod this for a game of *catenaccio*. Foggia went on a joyous romp, an orgy of goals that ended with them finishing ninth. Just three sides in the previous 25 years of Serie A had scored more than their tally of 58 goals and only the undefeated champions, AC Milan, scored more that season. They lost the last game of the season 8–2 to Milan, yet they had charmed so many observers that the team became known as *Foggia dei miracoli*. No translation is needed. They will be remembered forever.

FAHRENHEIT 4-2-3-1

Sir Stanley Matthews is perhaps the greatest English football player of all time. He was the inaugural inductee to the English Football Hall of Fame in 2002 and remains the only English football player to be knighted while still plying his trade. He kept playing throughout his 40s and in 1985 played his last ever competitive match at age 70. When he died in 2000, an estimated 100,000 people lined the streets of Stoke-on-Trent to pay their respects. Despite all this vast recognition, however, Sir Stanley played in a position that football fans under a certain age will probably never have heard of: outside right.

In the mid-20th century, teams would often take to the field lined up in a 4-2-4 formation. Four at the back, two in the middle, four up front. The outside right was, unsurprisingly, the outermost of the front four, on the right – a very advanced winger, if you like. With four forwards, football played well under the system was fast, attacking and exhilarating to watch. Nobody did it better than the Brazilians, who won the 1958 and 1970 World Cups playing that way; 4-4-2, the formation that has become the default formation for every level from kids' teams to pub sides to national squads, is a direct descendant. Invariably one of the two central midfielders remains slightly further back, but there is no such thing as an out-and-out defensive midfielder.

In the 1998/99 season, Manchester United were a swashbuckling, fearless side playing 4-4-2. The midfield paired Roy Keane with Paul Scholes; Scholes was the more attacking of the pair, but Keane still wrought trouble from box to box. Both missed the 1999 Champions League final due to suspension, but United's victorious European campaign was as joyously intrepid as football gets. In their 11 matches, there were 45 goals. Their run included a 3–2 win at Juventus in the semi-finals, and two unforgettable 3–3 draws with Barcelona in the group stages. Ferguson described the first of those as, 'the perfect football match – both teams trying to win with scant regard for the consequences. That's how football should be played.'

The legacy of this type of performance is that Ferguson is generally seen as a keeper of the attacking flame, which is, unfortunately, debatable. If Mourinho is the face of football's new pragmatism, then Ferguson is the face of the tactical change that occurred sometime around the turn of the century. Eighteen months after lifting that Champions League trophy, United surrendered the opportunity to defend it in a very similar match against Spanish opposition at Old Trafford. There should have been no shame in a numbing but ultimately unfortunate 3–2 defeat to Real Madrid, the eventual champions, but Ferguson seemed to lose his conviction in football 'with scant regard for the consequences' – a position which was only reinforced when Carlos Queiroz joined as his assistant manager in 2002. Almost overnight, it seemed, United's approach to the really big games became cagey at best. Previously the football

Manchester United played in such matches had been sexy; now it became Sextonian.[5]

Ferguson has experimented with all manner of tactics in his time – including a briefly thrilling 4-3-3-0 – yet football's increasingly defensive nature can be summed up in four chilling syllables: Four. Two. Three. One. Adopted by numerous teams, notably the national sides of Germany, Spain and the Netherlands (the same Spanish and Dutch sides that met in the 2010 World Cup final, described by Johan Cruyff as 'anti-football'), 4-2-3-1 has taken over from 4-4-2 as the vogue formation, having been introduced around the turn of the century; a Millennium Bug that has ruined football.

There is something insidious and deceitful about 4-2-3-1. If 4-4-2 is the bloke next door who will look you in the eye and drink you under the table, 4-2-3-1 is devious, a sneak and a phoney – not to be trusted. The problem is its four-pronged nature – formations should only really have three components: defence, midfield, attack. Football fans are generally simple folk, but now we have to deal with tactical developments that involve players getting between the lines, and other players getting between the lines between those lines. Even Einstein, who could follow a pretty complex argument when the mood took him, apparently, said that 'everything should be made as simple as possible'. Football, at its purest, should be straight-forward and carefree; whatever scaling up is inevitable in today's big-money game, we'd do well to remember that it is *a game*. Jimmy Greaves wasn't far off when he said that 'football tactics are rapidly

---

[5] If you don't remember the turgid nonsense served up by Dave Sexton in the late 1970s, you didn't miss much.

becoming as complicated as the chemical formula for splitting the atom'. If it carries on like this, soon everyone will be playing 1-1-1-1-1-1-1-1-1-1. It's far too confusing.

4-2-3-1 is a formation that exemplifies the cagey, defensive mindset of modern football managers. In a sense 4-2-3-1 is actually 6-3-1, for many sides employ two holding midfielders whose function is essentially or almost exclusively defensive. And it is getting worse. Mancini's Manchester City have been known to play three holding midfielders in a shape that is essentially 7-2-1, or 7-0-3. In 2010, Craig Levein, the Scotland manager, lined his team up in a 4-6-0 formation against the Czech Republic. 'The result was a display so negative that the BBC really should have shown it in black and white,' jibed the *Daily Telegraph*. The spirit of football took refuge in a darkened corner that night, and hugged its knees into the foetal position when Levein suggested that 'we might have to change our perception of what an interesting match is'

FAREWELL TO GENIUS

Jorge Valdano's 'shit on a stick' comment is one of the most famous in football in the last few years, yet there are a couple of misconceptions about it. One is that he said 'shit on a stick'. It was actually 'shit hanging from a stick'; maybe it will appear alongside 'all that glitters is not gold' and 'you're a big man but you're out of shape' when the list of 100 Greatest Misquotes appears on Channel 4. The other is that he was referring exclusively to negative and/or incompetent football. In fact, Valdano's primary attack was on one of modern football's more sacred cows: teamwork.

Sid Lowe's 2007 *Guardian* article cites an English translation of what Valdano originally wrote in the Spanish newspaper *Marca,* after that year's dismal Champions League semi-final between Chelsea and Liverpool:

Football is made up of subjective feeling, of suggestion – and, in that, Anfield is unbeatable. Put a shit hanging from a stick in the middle of this passionate, crazy stadium and there are people who will tell you it's a work of art. It's not: it's a shit hanging from a stick.

Chelsea and Liverpool are the clearest, most exaggerated example of the way football is going: very intense, very collective, very tactical, very physical, and very direct. But, a short pass? Noooo. A feint? Noooo. A change of pace? Noooo. A one-two? A nutmeg? A back-heel? Don't be ridiculous. None of that. The extreme control and seriousness with which both teams played the semi-final neutralised any creative licence, any moments of exquisite skill.

If Didier Drogba was the best player in the first match it was purely because he was the one who ran the fastest, jumped the highest and crashed into people the hardest. Such extreme intensity wipes away talent, even leaving a player of Joe Cole's class disoriented. If football is going the way Chelsea and Liverpool are taking it, we had better be ready to wave goodbye to any expression of the cleverness and talent we have enjoyed for a century.

The collective has almost subsumed the individual, and football is in danger of banning flair and improvisation in the name of tactics. This complaint isn't entirely new – in 1984, Hugh McIlvanney bemoaned the 'swirl of incoherent energy that is the predominant language of the First Division'. At Cambridge in 1992, the manager John Beck, who had the groundsman grow the grass long in the corners of the pitch to hold up long balls, substituted striker Steve Claridge after 20 minutes of a 1–1 draw with Ipswich for the heinous crime of turning inside and passing the ball. (The pair then had a fight in the break; after the game, Beck told his team that 'it's a shame you bastards didn't show the same passion as he did at half-time'.) As with so many of the things we bemoan in this book, it's a question of degree. Individuality will always be the soul of all sport, even team sports. In the past we knew great players by fairytale nicknames like 'The Wizard of the Dribble' (Matthews), 'Cosmic Kite' (Maradona) or 'Beauty of the Night' (as former Juventus owner Gianni Agnelli christened Zbigniew Boniek, because he always sparkled during European Cup evening games). Today Andrés Iniesta is known as 'the Illusionist', but the often more celebrated Cristiano Ronaldo is known in the Real Madrid dressing room rather less romantically as 'the Machine'.

Too much teamwork brings a joylessness to the game, a tactical straitjacket that precludes players from expressing themselves. They become chess pieces with a limited repertoire of moves (witness Gareth Barry's existential angst outside of his own half as one of Mancini's defensive midfielders in 2010/11) rather than real-life action heroes. To witness self-expression and creativity is to see football at its most soulful, yet there is increasing snobbery about managers telling players to 'just go out and play', as if this reflects a misunderstanding of the complexity of the game rather than a firm grasp of its majesty in the care of an unleashed player. Valeriy Lobanovsky, the legendary manager of Dynamo Kiev (with whom he won no fewer than 30 Soviet, Ukrainian and European trophies), as well as both the Soviet and Ukrainian national football teams, demanded a kind of Eastern Bloc Total Football from his players: 'I don't like players having positions. There's no such thing as a striker, a midfielder, a defender. There are only footballers and they should be able to do everything on the pitch.' Yet he placed huge value on an individual's distinct set of skills and during his time at Dynamo Kiev nurtured some of the recent past's most exciting players, including Andriy Shevchenko (incidentally, nicknamed the 'Eastern Wind'). The balance between the individual and collective is one of the most precarious in football, and at the moment it seems to have drifted too far towards the latter. Teamwork may be an essentially worthy thing, admirable even, but if taken too far it is a betrayal of the reason we all started playing sport in the first place. If we are not careful, footballers will become automata. And whether you say 'automayta' or 'automatta', it really will be time to call the whole thing off.

The 2010 World Cup stood out in this regard: most of the world's best players had extremely poor tournaments. Cristiano Ronaldo, Wayne Rooney, Samuel Eto'o, Kaká, Fernando Torres, Didier Drogba and Steven Gerrard – all of whom had been in the top 11 of the previous year's Ballon d'Or – had various shades of shocker. Even Lionel Messi, although threatening throughout, failed to score a goal. It was rare to see a player who wanted to express himself and seize the day, which made Kevin-Prince Boateng's performances for Ghana one of the highlights of the tournament. Nobody in the world, except Prince Boateng and maybe his mum, would suggest he is one of the best players in the world, yet he was one of the most striking performers at that World Cup. Most of all, he looked like he was actually *enjoying* himself. That such a thing is worthy of note neatly sums up how much football has changed at the highest levels; footballers must look like they're working hard and knuckling down, *getting the job done*.

Football should be art. Just before the 2010 World Cup started, *Daily Telegraph* writer Tom Horan theorised that: 'If art is an attempt by man to recreate recognisable patterns of his emotional life, to replicate and mirror aspects of the human condition through an artificial form, then football definitely does these things.' Former Blackpool defender Paul Gardner was briefer: 'It is an athletic ballet.' Try watching Andrés Iniesta and arguing otherwise. One of the joys for Manchester United fans in recent times has been to watch Dimitar Berbatov, the point at which football and art meet in sublime, almost sensual, moments of footballing genius. There are legitimate arguments as to Berbatov's effectiveness, which ultimately led to him dropping behind not just Wayne Rooney but also Javier Hernandez and even Danny Welbeck in 2011, yet he provided so many moments to remember: moments of Berberotica, where the tedious concerns about winning were temporarily rendered pointless by the stunning rush of seeing somebody achieve the barely imaginable with a football. This, surely, is why we watch the game. Berbatov doesn't so much control the ball as seduce it with a Velcro first touch, to be his for ever more – or until he decides to cast it off in the direction of Darron Gibson.[6]

---

[6] This is not to suggest that players should be allowed to indulge themselves as they see fit. There are few sights more tedious in football than watching players like Cristiano Ronaldo and Nani on one of those days when their sole interest is in doing everything themselves. Indeed, some people feel that Manchester United were beaten by Barcelona in the 2009 Champions League final because Ronaldo, knowing it would be his last match for the club, decided to try and win the thing single-handedly.

Berbatov is a player capable of greatness, if not a great player, and the obvious downside of an increased focus on the collective is a diminishing number of star players. There are, of course, some magnificent footballers around, but how many of the current crop will enter the pantheon? Messi, Ronaldo, Xavi and Andrés Iniesta are probably the only guarantees, although you could also make a case for Gerard Piqué, Rio Ferdinand, Kaká, Eto'o, Arjen Robben and, if you are taking current players who are a bit past it, Ronaldinho. There are arguably no great (in the strictest sense of the word) players currently at work in the Premier League. The fact that Gareth Bale and Scott Parker (two admirable players, but players whose best assets are, essentially, speed and stamina) won the individual awards for best player in 2010/11 supports that perception.

This is a subjective issue, of course, yet it feels like there were more greats in the past. Wind back ten years and you had Zinedine Zidane, Ronaldo, Rivaldo, Luís Figo, Roy Keane, Paolo Maldini, Pavel Nedvěd, Andriy Shevchenko, Thierry Henry, Gabriel Batistuta, Raúl, Fernando Redondo, Marcel Desailly, Oliver Kahn, Alessandro Nesta and Roberto Carlos. Wind back to 1991 and there was Marco van Basten, Lothar Matthäus, Andreas Brehme, Romàrio, Michael Laudrup, Peter Schmeichel, Ruud Gullit, Jürgen Klinsmann, Jean-Pierre Papin, Dejan Savićević, Paul Gascoigne, Gheorghe Hagi, Paul McGrath, Franco Baresi, Roberto Baggio, Hristo Stoichkov and, of course, Paolo Maldini again.

MEN FROM MARS

In 1906, 22-year-old Max Seeburg signed for Chelsea, the club having been formed the previous year. He played there for two years before moving to Tottenham Hotspur for the 1908/09 season. His name may not ring a bell for many football fans any more, but he earns his place in history as being the first continental European to play in English football. Some 70-odd years later, Spurs grabbed the headlines with another foreign acquisition – two, in fact, this time from Argentina. Fresh from winning the 1978 World Cup, Osvaldo Ardiles and Ricardo Villa, two talented midfielders, were brought to Britain for a combined total of £750,000. Swiftly renamed Ossie and Ricky by the fans, Ardiles and Villa became Tottenham legends, thrilling those who saw them with their sparkling attacking play.

At 3pm on Saturday August 15th 1992, getting on for a century after Seeburg had joined Chelsea, the Premier League kicked off for the first time ever. Even then, however, foreign players were a bit of a rarity in English football. There were only 11 of them named in the starting line-ups for those inaugural matches: Peter Schmeichel (Danish, Manchester United), Jan Stejskal (Czech, QPR), Roland Nilsson (Swedish, Sheffield Wednesday), Michel Vonk (Dutch, Manchester City), John Jensen (Danish, Arsenal), Gunnar Halle (Norwegian, Oldham Athletic), Eric Cantona (French, Leeds United), Anders Limpar (Swedish, Arsenal), Hans Segers (Dutch, Wimbledon), Andrei Kanchelskis (Russian, Manchester United) and Tony Dorigo (Australian, Leeds).

Human beings are supposed to be afraid of the unknown, yet a bit of mystery makes life's tapestry so much richer. With the exception of the identity of the latest person to gain a super-injunction, there are few mysteries in football. Certainly the most charming of all – seeing unknown teams and players who wow us with the shock of the new – has all but gone. There are a number of reasons for this: increased television coverage, the internet, computer games like *Championship Manager* and, naturally, globalisation.

There are now over 300 foreign players represented in the Premier League, from 66 different countries. Of course this is ultimately a good thing, and English football is so much richer for its diversity, but that has come at a price. It's easy to recall the thrill of discovering a completely unknown talent at a World Cup: not just one-hit wonders like Josimar and Salvatore Schillaci, but even the greats. In 1986, most English people would have heard of Diego Maradona, but few would have seen him play beyond the odd highlights reel. The same goes for Pelé in 1970, Johan Cruyff and Franz Beckenbauer in 1974 and Lothar Matthäus in 1990.

Often whole teams could spring a surprise. Up until the early 1950s, England had never been beaten on home soil by a country from outside of the British Isles – Ireland's 2–0 victory in a friendly match at Goodison Park in 1949 was the only defeat they had suffered to opposition from outside the United Kingdom. On November 25th 1953, in front of 105,000 fans at Wembley, Walter Winterbottom's England prepared to take on Hungary. The Mighty Magyars were not without some profile: they were reigning Olympic champions and ranked No. 1 in the world (England were No. 3). Yet not one Englishman in the FA, the national side or the terraces seriously thought that the Hungarians would be any kind of threat. They had never heard of these players, after all, and their approach and tactics were foreign, in every sense of the word. On seeing the Hungarians' low-profile, lightweight boots as the teams headed out on to the pitch, England's great central defender, Billy Wright, turned to teammate Stan Mortensen and said, 'We should be alright here, Stan, they haven't got the proper kit.'

What followed was a brutal shredding of England's naivety. Hungary scored within a minute and ran out 6–3 winners. The late Sir Bobby Robson, then 20 years old and an inside forward at Fulham, watched the game from the stands; reflecting on it later, he expressed the combination of shock, awe and revisionist thinking that this unknown team had forced upon an unsuspecting nation:

> We saw a style of play, a system of play that we had never seen before. None of these players meant anything to us. We didn't know about Puskás. All these fantastic players, they were men from Mars as far as we were concerned. They were coming to England, England had never been beaten at Wembley – this would be a 3–0, 4–0, maybe even 5–0 demolition of a small country who were just coming into European football.
>
> They called Puskás the 'Galloping Major' because he was in the army – how could this guy serving for the Hungarian army come to Wembley and rifle us to defeat? But the way they played, their technical brilliance and expertise – our WM formation was kyboshed in 90 minutes of football. The game had a profound effect, not just on myself but on all of us… That one game alone changed our thinking. We thought we would demolish this team – England at Wembley, we are the masters, they are the pupils. It was absolutely the other way.

Up to 40 years later, European club matches still carried the most seductive mystique, with trips to places like Russia and Poland to play against sides that journalists were contractually obliged to describe as a 'crack Eastern European outfit'. It's almost impossible to find that these days, although the most charming element of Russia's progress to the semi-finals at Euro 2008 was that they were, to most of us, relatively unknown. All bar one of the 23-man squad still played in Russia and, although Zenit St. Petersburg had won the UEFA Cup that season, the side were still young, fresh and new. Their quarter-final victory over Holland was revelatory for all sorts of reasons, not least the apparent emergence of a series of new stars, in particular Andriy Arshavin, Yuri Zhirkov and Roman Pavlyuchenko. That all three have since had fairly underwhelming spells in London (at, respectively, Arsenal, Chelsea and Spurs) does not impinge upon the vivid memory of that night.

The speed, however, with which those Russian players went from playing in their domestic league to turning out for (at the time at least comparatively) wealthy Premier League teams speaks of an environment in which the only thing that dominant teams are doing with scant regard for the consequences any more is buying up talent from elsewhere. A sad offshoot of globalised football is that there is very little scope for so-called golden generations to emerge and develop into seriously competitive sides. As soon as a relatively unknown team does make an impact, it invariably loses its star – often home-grown – players to the riches of Spain, Italy or England. We've already talked about the ruthless ambition shown by players hankering after a bigger stage, but we should be mindful of the extent to which anyone is prepared to defend the right of the rich and powerful to exert such a pull over others.

In the 1970s, Ajax's Total Footballers were able to win three European Cups in a row. A very similar group of players emerged in the early 1990s and won the Champions League in 1995. A year later they had lost six of the 16-man match-day squad; within three years they had lost 11 of them – an entire team of footballers. Seven of those players would go on to play for Barcelona. The same was true of the spellbinding Red Star Belgrade side who won the European Cup in 1991. Their situation was slightly different because of the war in Yugoslavia, but the basic point remains. Within 12 months they had lost their five star players: Dejan Savićević (AC Milan), Robert Prosinečki (Real Madrid), Darko Pančev (Internazionale), Vladimir Jugović (Sampdoria) and Siniša Mihajlović (Roma). The same thing happened at Valencia after they reached consecutive Champions League finals in 2000 and 2001, Bayer Leverkusen after their thrilling run to the Champions League final in 2002, and Porto after they won the competition in 2004. The latter's name had barely been engraved on the trophy before the manager José Mourinho, as well as leading players Deco, Ricardo Carvalho and Paulo Ferreira had left the club.

All these clubs had the potential to disturb the old order of European football, yet globalisation and market forces denied them that chance. Even teams that threaten not to shatter the earth but simply to give it a firm rap cannot avoid falling victim to this process. Around 2003, a group of promising young players emerged from the youth ranks at Hibernian, helping them to the League Cup final in 2004, a trophy the club went on to win in 2007. That year they lost Scott Brown to Celtic, and Kevin Thomson and Steven Whittaker to Rangers, having already sold Derek Riordan to Celtic for a cut-price fee a few months before his contract expired in 2006. He'd refused a contract extension at the end of the 2004/05 season, when he was named the Scottish PFA Young Player of the Year. In England, between playing the last match of the 2010/11 Premier League season and the close of that summer's transfer window, Blackpool lost the services of hugely influential midfielders Charlie Adam (Liverpool) and David Vaughan (Sunderland), as well as top scorer D.J. Campbell (QPR). Before he'd left Old Trafford on the final day of the season, defender Ian Evatt told reporters: 'We will lose this group of lads; I'm sure the vultures will come circling to buy them all. It will be very difficult to return to this level.' In football's closed shop, it doesn't pay to be an intrepid outsider.

Golden generations can still thrive, but generally only at the very biggest clubs. Manchester United's Alan Hansen generation (a term adopted by the players themselves) – Ryan Giggs, Paul Scholes, David Beckham, Gary Neville, Phil Neville and Nicky Butt – won 119 major honours between them. The Barcelona team that started the 2011 Champions League final had seven home-grown players: six Spaniards plus Argentina's Lionel Messi, who came to Spain from Argentine side Newell's Old Boys at the age of 12 when Barcelona offered treatment for his growth-hormone deficiency.

In so many respects Barcelona has an exemplary youth structure. Their players are educated at La Masia, the club's training facilities, in such a way that they can move seamlessly through the ranks until they eventually reach the first team. Yet Barcelona are far from spotless. The ease with which the rich clubs pick apart other talented teams, colonising the time and space in which to build a generation-defining side, is astonishing, but it is in their dealings with youth players that these clubs have really sullied the game. The global game has led to the desperate poaching of teenage talent, and Barcelona have been as widely criticised as any club in that regard.

In 2004, when they poached 12-year-old Dennis Krol, his former club Bayer Leverkusen claimed that Barcelona had offered his father €7,000 a month. In the same year, the father of a 12-year-old at River Plate claimed Barcelona had offered him and his wife €120,000 a year to move with their child to Spain. There was discontent in Australia a year later when Barcelona took a six-year-old on trial. In 2010 Arsenal's 17-year-old Benik Afobe said that he had rejected an approach from Barcelona. 'They spoke to my Dad,' he said. 'I was flattered.'

Barcelona have had their own counter-complaints about Arsenal, who poached Cesc Fàbregas in 2003. When the London club lured French teenager, Jon Toral, in May 2011 the Barcelona chairman said: 'We don't like it that clubs come in with offers of money just before boys turn 16. There are two philosophies: ours is to invest in [our academy] and the other is to fish all over Europe for kids like Arsenal do. It's legal, but a little immoral '

The moral dubiousness of clubs' willingness to poach players barely into puberty, never mind out of it, is indicative of the broader treatment of footballers as commodities rather than people. The phrase 'marquee signing' has become unpleasantly prevalent in modern football. The concept of the marquee player has even been formalised in the A-League, Australia's premier competition, where each club is permitted one marquee player who is exempt from the league's wage cap.

Of course, the signing of big-name players has always attracted attention – when Ardiles and Villa joined Spurs back in 1978, the fans gave them a ticker-tape reception on their debut. That response, however, was born out of fans' excitement at the prospect of watching the exotic, talented duo play football. The marquee signing in the 21st century is selected according to the additional revenue that the club see coming their way, whether from ticket sales, shirt sales, new fan bases or endorsements.

Real Madrid are perhaps the most extreme example of the use of marquee players in amassing a team of *galácticos* under Florentino Pérez's first presidency between 2000 and 2006. In 2003, David Beckham arrived at the club from Manchester United for a reported £25 million. This was the highest-profile player in the world joining arguably the highest-profile team in the world. 'Getting him onto the squad of Real Madrid is not just a case of betting on a sports plan,' said Miguel Angel Sastre, Professor of Corporate Organisation at the Universidad Complutense de Madrid, and it did not take long for many to realise it was not necessarily a deal that was all about improving the team. 'Purely from a football perspective,' commented Scott Rosner, a lecturer at the Wharton School of the University of Pennsylvania (a business school, incidentally, not a sports one), 'Beckham is a terrific player, but Real Madrid is so good that Beckham may not make the starting line-up. His real value to the team is in the branding of the club worldwide. He is yet another star that Real Madrid can sell as they try to enhance their world image.'

Modern players must perform for the club both on the pitch and in the megastore: in Beckham's first season in Madrid, Real's revenue from club merchandise soared by 67%. They also became the richest club in the world; in doing so they overtook Beckham's old team, Manchester United. Club merchandise, once a sideline that supporters themselves often organised, is becoming increasingly central to club strategy. Within minutes of the announcement of

Craig Bellamy's return to Liverpool in August 2011, it was possible to order a 'Bellamy 39' shirt from the club's online store. The Welsh striker isn't quite in Beckham's league, but such swiftness meant that any interest whipped up by the move's last-minute, surprise nature (particularly during the relatively quiet last hours of this deadline day) could be capitalised upon.

Such behaviour has bred a cynicism in fans, rather than celebration. It has been fortunately rare, but unfortunately true, that fans and commentators alike have discussed the phenomenon of buying inadequate players from potentially lucrative markets simply for commercial reasons. This is impossible to prove, of course, but there are a few players in recent times whose signings have raised eyebrows but whose performances on the field – when, indeed, they have got on to the field – have not quickened a single pulse. Perhaps the most infamous was Manchester United's Chinese striker Dong Fangzhuo, who only made three appearances in the four years between 2004 and 2008 that he spent at the club. Two of those were in dead rubbers; the other was a League Cup tie at home to Coventry. He now plays for Mika F.C. in the Armenian Premier League. (Even most Armenians don't watch that.)

Though he wasn't talking about Dong's short-lived English career, Richard Arnold, the Manchester United Commercial Director, acknowledged in 2011 that 'Asia is very important for anyone who is a genuine global phenomenon'. In recent years the club has splintered its commercial department to target different world regions, signing individual media deals, and in 2011 United were given the go-ahead on a £635 million share offering on the Singapore stock exchange. The nod came not long after US logistics firm DHL paid £40 million simply to have its name adorn United's training kits in the hope of seeing the brand pop up on screens all over the world. Even in the Premier League, most clubs' shirt sponsors don't pay that kind of money. It all feels a long way from Newton Heath.

THE IRRATIONAL NOSTALGIA CARD

Amidst the cynicism of clubs, the caginess of managers and the self-regard of players – and in a wildly avaricious commercial environment only too happy to trample the game underfoot if there's a profit in it – it seems fair to ask what's left for the fan in the stand? The answer is: not much. Just as the joy is being sucked out of the game itself, so the tools of the trade are acquiring the bland plasticity of mass production. Not even the humble home strip, that swathe of polyester with which we identify ourselves as part of a clan, has escaped the clawing fingers of the modern money game.

In some respects, nostalgia is life's big ruse – a comfort blanket for when the present looks dodgy and the future even dodgier. Often nostalgia doesn't stand up to the mildest scrutiny, but we're about to play the Irrational Nostalgia Card, if we may. Football fans are, almost by definition, a nostalgic bunch, their 'earts wooed by their 'istory. And that's the point here. You don't need to think too deeply in any sense for it to work. A memory box could just carry a list of names and it would still give you an almighty Proustian rush.

There has been, as the rest of this book explores, a demonstrable change in the game since the inception of the Premier League in 1992, and sometimes the things that appear to matter the least need addressing, too. Replica football kits are made of material that makes you sweat even at brisk walking pace and which clings unflatteringly to even a relatively flat belly, yet people put them on every weekend, in public. And surely nobody – *nobody* – would credibly argue that the kits up to the very, very early 1990s were not vastly superior to those of the last 20 years.

Broadly speaking, there are two types of human being: those who preferred the virginal shirts of the 1960s and 1970s, and those who favour the kits of the 1980s, with the flourishes added by manufacturers' and sponsors' logos. And this retro-kit market is a vast, global affair – unsigned kits can fetch well over £200 – and the magnificent classicfootballshirts.co.uk[7] covers most bases in that regard.

We all have our favourite kits from the past. Denmark's 1986 number stands out, an appropriately futuristic outfit, designed by Hummel, which was both halved and pinstriped. (It's better than it sounds.) There is also England's classic 1982 Admiral kit – so effortlessly chic that not even the sight of Pete Doherty wearing it could tarnish its coolness, and a far cry from the 2010 alternative red outfit that Tom Meighan, the lead singer of Kasabian, was signed up to wear at one of the band's gigs in Paris. There's the AC Milan Mediolanum-sponsored strip that was worn by their three Dutchmen, Marco van Basten, Ruud Gullit and Frank Rijkaard, and then of course the France 1984 top, as vivid and as graceful as the midfield quartet sporting it. Italia 90 had some fantastic kits, including probably the last iconic England top. There was also Cameroon's, a monstrous lion stuck on the breast of a

---

[7] Scientific studies have shown that it is physically impossible to spend more than 90 seconds on that site without a big dumb grin breaking across your face.

striking green-and-white effort; the simple, glamorous sheen of Italy's blue top; and West Germany's, with black, red and yellow lines taking a long-winded route across the centre of the kit. It shouldn't have worked, but it did.

By 1992 or so, when design tools got carried away with their design tools and started treating kits like a canvas for an ersatz Jackson Pollock effort, all bets were off. It was also the year Adidas marginalised the majestic trefoil in favour of having three stripes. There have been some shockers since then – including Hull's tiger strip of 1993, David Seaman's disgusting goalkeeper top at Euro 96, and the kit that France wore during their World Cup-winning campaign of 1998, a cynical update of the classic 1984 strip that was as big an act of cultural vandalism as the remake of *The Vanishing*.

If many modern kits have been uneasy on the eye, then some have also left a bad taste in the mouth. The frequency with which clubs began to release kits, cynically exploiting parents powerless to resist their children's pleas for the latest top, was so extreme that regulations had to be put in place. When Tottenham Hotspur decided to start changing all three strips every single year, they even had the cheek to announce the decision by saying that they'd noticed fans in the stands were wearing lots of older shirts, which they had taken as a subliminal demand for more new shirts to choose from. The idea that fans were wearing shirts they already had because they couldn't afford (or didn't want) a new one apparently didn't figure in that board meeting.

You can never go wrong with a Brazil kit, even today, but our favourites were the 1986 and 1990 efforts, in a slightly faded yellow, designed by Topper. *Topper*. How cool is that? Most kits these days are made by a select few companies: Adidas, Nike, Puma and Umbro. The same quadropoly generally persists in the area of boot-making, a market that has a new balance – one that doesn't involve New Balance, or other nostalgia-inducing companies like Sondico, Lotto or Diadora. Market forces make such domination inevitable, but the 1998 World Cup final cast a sinister shadow over the commercial interests behind footballers' outfits. Nike – who had signed a record $160m deal with the Confederação Brasileira de Futebol two years earlier – were accused of pressurising Brazil's star striker, Ronaldo, to play in that match despite suffering an epileptic fit earlier that day. They were fully cleared, but it is sad that football had reached the stage where anyone was even suspicious.

Call us rheumy-eyed wasters, but old boots were cooler – they were black, for a start, none of this fluorescent look-at-me nonsense from players whose greatest achievement in the game is to take an accurate corner once a month – and so were old footballs. Nothing will ever match the retro classics of the Adidas Telstar and especially the Adidas Tango, the balls used at the World Cups between 1970 and 1982. Unlike the trusty Mitre Delta or the chilling Mitre Mouldmaster – the one with the rough, basketball-style texture that invariably left a stinging kiss on your inner thigh during PE lessons – these weren't readily available to Joe Public. They cost loads, and you'd have needed to save your pocket money for about four lifetimes to buy one. So it took two to Tango: you to nag, nag, nag away at your parents, and them to blow about half their weekly wage on one. Some chance.

Modern footballs may be more readily available to the common child, but that's about all they have going for them. Their main problem is not the way they look, but the way they move. The beach-ball effect has never been more extreme than at the 2010 World Cup, when Adidas's Jabulani made a fool of pretty much every goalkeeper in the tournament. (Brazil's Júlio César lambasted it as a 'supermarket ball'.) Generally speaking, a football should hold its line. Like the lady, it should not be for turning. When the *Guardian*'s website held a poll for the goal of the 2010/11 season, the winner was Freddy Guarín's extraordinary 40-yarder for FC Porto against fellow Portuguese side Maritimo, scored using the Jabulani. It was a remarkable goal, yet the ball changed direction at least six times en route, wobbling one way and then the other to befuddle the goalkeeper.

Guarín is a fine player, but there is no way in the world he meant that to happen. The preponderance of footballs that have a mind of their own has removed a level of trust in the technique of players who exploit them. We suspect the likes of Cristiano Ronaldo and Didier Drogba are exceptional free-kick takers, with, in Ronaldo's case, unusually rubbery ankles, but we don't really *know* they are in the way that we did with the likes of the great Brazilians Zico and Didi or indeed Alan Suddick, the English player who was famed in the 1960s and 70s for his 'banana' free kicks. Today's balls put an asterisk against the dead-ball achievements of modern footballers.

There are, of course, certain advantages to modern footballs compared to some of those used in the past, which were often no more than glorified medicine balls. After West Bromwich Albion forward Jeff Astle (who scored the winner in the 1968 FA Cup final against Everton) dropped dead at 59 years old in 2002, the coroner recorded a verdict of death by industrial injury, saying that the trauma caused by heading the old leather footballs had led to degenerative brain damage, and ultimately, the player's death. His wife Lorraine said Jeff had described heading the ball on a wet day as like 'heading a bag of bricks'.

In that, as in so many respects, footballers have it easier these days. There are, for example, very few glitches in the pitches any more. Just look at the bowling greens they get to play on, mainly a consequence of increased craftsmanship and undersoil heating. The pitch at the new Wembly stadium, which took about as long to sort out as a male model's hair, was a rare example of a modern bad pitch – yet with none of the charm of old. It was not the sort of mud-heap that reduced a match to an endearing lottery, but at its worst was a kind of football Temazepam, draining the life from both sides' attempt to pass the ball at pace. Properly shocking pitches – like at Derby's Baseball Ground, which was so bad in the 1970s that it was not unknown for a man to come on to paint the penalty spot during the match – bring back happy memories of a purer time, when the game simply had to go on. The wear and tear of the season was almost always visible by Christmas, with wet weather mixing up some filthy pitches. It makes some of the great goals scored on them even more brilliant.

CHAPTER 3
IN A £EAGU€ OF THEIR OWN

Jules Rimet, the French lawyer who created the World Cup, was an idealist of magnificent proportions: his main interest in football, which he never played, was its power to restore chivalry and bring world peace. The game's ability to unite people across any differences would, he believed, create a world where 'men will be able to meet in confidence without hatred in their hearts and without an insult on their lips'. Football could not help but create comrades of us all.

* * *

In 1954, when Wolverhampton Wanderers capped off an unbeaten run of 'floodlit friendlies' at Molineux with a 3–2 win over Hungarian side Honvéd (in which they came back in the second half from two–nil down with the instruction, 'Get out there and play your normal game'), the *Daily Mail* called them 'Champions of the World'. The habitually understated reaction of the British press prompted action from *L'Équipe* editor Gabriel Hanot. 'Before we declare that Wolverhampton are invincible,' he wrote, 'let them go to Moscow and Budapest. And there are other internationally renowned clubs: AC Milan and Real Madrid to name but two. A club world championship, or at least a European one – larger, more meaningful and more prestigious than the Mitropa Cup and more original than a competition for national teams – should be launched.'

* * *

Decades earlier, William McGregor, director of Aston Villa – one of the clubs that had threatened a breakaway competition in order to force the FA to permit the professionalisation of the English game – broached the subject of a formal league with a rather less romantic letter to his counterparts at clubs round about the north-west of England. 'I beg to tender the following suggestion,' he wrote. 'That ten or twelve of the most prominent clubs in England combine to arrange home-and-away fixtures each season. Every year it is becoming more and more difficult for football clubs of any standing to meet their friendly engagements and even arrange friendly matches. The consequence is that at the last moment, through cup-tie interference, clubs are compelled to take on teams who will not attract the public.'

* * *

On the face of it, the origins of some of the world's football competitions could hardly be more different, variously and more or less implicitly involving the human condition, glory and recognition, structure and accountability. Yet only in the case of the Football League is there even a hint of the scent of banknotes – McGregor's slightly pompous concern with attracting the public. In the modern game, money has waltzed in like an overzealous *Changing Rooms* interior designer, making drastic and unseemly alterations.

GREED IS GOOD: THE PREMIER LEAGUE

As first dates go, August 15th 1992 was pretty good. It was the first day of the Premier League, and the promise of a brave new world seemed genuine. There were shocks (Manchester United losing at Sheffield United, Norwich coming from 2–0 down to win 4–2 at title favourites Arsenal), breathtaking goals (Mark Robins for Norwich at Highbury, two majestic long-range strikes from Alan Shearer on his Blackburn debut), thrillers (Arsenal v Norwich, as well as Crystal Palace 3–3 Blackburn), and even a nice did-he-mean-that moment when Wimbledon defender Warren Barton's floated cross from deep on the right went over John Lukic and into the net away to the champions Leeds United. Great players make their own luck, but also their own judgment – when something like this happens, we trust in genius and say it was deliberate (the Romanian maestro Gheorghe Hagi did something similar in the World Cup of 1994 and Brazil's Ronaldinho repeated the feat in the same competition in 2002). This being poor old Warren Barton, most people thought it was a fluke.

We digress. It was a lovely late summer's day, and all seemed pretty well with the world of English football. *Match of the Day* was covering league football for the first time in four years. Des Lynam was back. It was the dawning of a new era, yet it also felt like football had come home.

The first date went well, the second even better, but the

romance quickly evaporated. Nineteen years later we are still together, but trapped in a loveless marriage with very little in common. We have many differences, but they all boil down to one persistent incompatibility: one of us loves football, the other loves money. While we might look at the numbers – in the 2010/11 season, more than 13 million tickets were sold for Premier League games – and reflect on people's remarkably resilient love of the game in the face of vast changes to match days (see Chapter Five), the Premier League website boasts that it is 'the world's most watched league and the most lucrative'. Since when did either of these matter? It's like boasting about how much you earn and how many followers you have on Twitter, craven measures that should mean nothing to football, not to mention the obvious pitfalls of *ad populum* logic. *The X Factor* gets an audience of more than ten million people every Saturday for four months of the year, but that doesn't mean they're not watching the music industry gone wrong.

When the Premier League was set up in 1992, the eminent football writer Brian Glanville dubbed it the 'Greed-is-Good League'. How right he was. The clubs didn't even bother coming up with a creditable cover story, concocting (with the help of the FA) a tale so risible – the envisaged 18-team league was designed to leave players fitter and fresher for England duty, apparently – that even Graham Taylor spotted the pound signs in people's eyes. Under this new Gordon Gekko regime, football supporters (like everything else) have become, first and foremost, revenue. It was almost a surprise to discover that the Premier League's new HQ was to be based alongside the rest of the FA in their then home on Lancaster Gate, and not in an office on Wall Street. In the ensuing years a host of corporate interests have graffitied their names on to the top flight, at ever greater cost. While the 72 teams of the Football League share a sponsorship deal with the energy company npower worth £7 million per season between 2010/11 and 2012/13, the Premier League has a deal with Barclays worth £27.5 million per year, to be shared between 20 clubs.

Financed so handsomely, the Premier League has succumbed to the same weaknesses of character as its players and descended into dismal arrogance. As well as boasting that it is the most lucrative of the world's leagues, the Premier League website also puffs out its chest and says that it is 'widely regarded as the elite club competition in world football'. If any of us had a pound, or even a penny, for every time the Premier League has been called the best in the world over the last decade, *The Sunday Times* Rich List would be in need of urgent revision. Such tedious hype is probably inevitable – Barclays, or whoever it is next, doesn't pay all that money to christen a league that humbly acknowledges that it has its good days and its bad – but it looks very much like the excessively loud assertion of the chronically insecure. If we value a league on the basis of its competitiveness and unpredictability, the quality of the football, the attacking nature of the football, and the strength of the fan culture, it is hard to say, convincingly, that the Premier League is the best in the world.

Many, however, will focus on a single criterion, which allows you to have your cake, eat it and then call it the best damned slice of sponge on the planet. In May 2009, the fact that nine of the last 12 Champions League semi-finalists had been English was given as evidence of the Premier League's superiority. Two years later, when only one of the previous eight semi-finalists had been English – putting the Premier

League on a par with France's Ligue 1 and Serie A – it's all gone quiet over there. Manchester United have now been soundly beaten, humiliated, even, in two finals against Barcelona; in 2011, Spain is palpably the home of the best team in Europe, and probably the second best. Confronted by reality, the justification is simply and swiftly changed: the Premier League is the best because it is the most competitive.

The essence of any competition is, well, its competition, and it is very obviously the case that the top flight of English football is nowhere near as competitive as it once was. The gulf between first and last is remarkable. That the title has been won by only four different teams in 19 years – and that one of those teams has won it 12 times – suggests the league is about as competitive as a 60-yard dash with Usain Bolt. In pure football terms, the Premier League has failed. A couple of years ago, with a new season about to start, Sky showed an advert with a theoretically cute ginger kid waxing wide-eyed at the thought of what lay ahead. 'Anything can happen!' he said. If nothing else, you have to admire the brass neck of it, because one of the saddest things about the Premier League is that the first-day-of-the-season optimism has all but vanished. The season used to start as a blank canvas, each match a brushstroke adding light here, shade there. Now it's a simple join-the-dots job.

In February 2011, bottom-of-the-table Wolverhampton Wanderers completed a hat-trick of home victories over the eventual top three of Manchester United, Chelsea and Manchester City, prompting the kind of giddy response usually only seen when an alcoholic happens upon a half-eaten liqueur chocolate in a moment of weakness. 'You can always expect a game between top versus bottom in

England,' wrote Alan Hansen, in the *Daily Telegraph*. No. No, you can't. The 2010/11 season was the most competitive in years, but the bar had been dropping lower ever since 1992.[8] United's away record – five wins in 19 – was uncharacteristically diabolical, but neither it nor Wolves' impressive wins really said much about equilibrium. The rest of the top four still picked up points away from home in quantities that would have seemed abnormal 20 years ago. Away games used to be fiendishly difficult, yet it is now a minor shock if the title contenders even *draw* away to teams in the bottom half of the table. Arsenal, who finished fourth in 2010/11, took 31 points from their 19 away games – only two fewer than Manchester United's great Treble-winning side managed in 1998/99. 'Some dictionaries define a league as "an association of sporting clubs that organises matches between member teams of a similar standard",' the *Guardian*'s David Lacey wrote that year. 'If this is the case, then the Premier League offends the Trade Descriptions Act on an annual basis.'

On the topic of competitiveness, Spain's La Liga usually makes a comforting comparison: Barcelona and Real Madrid are miles ahead of the chasing pack – 25 points clear of third-placed Valencia in 2009/10, and 21 points ahead the year after. Barcelona won by three clear goals or more on 13 occasions in 2010/11, Real Madrid on 12 occasions, and both averaged around 2.5 points per game. But the Premier League is kidding itself if it thinks that many of its mid- and lower-table clubs can afford to entertain any grander notions than their

---

[8] Using research from footballeconomics.com, *The Sports Economist* blog developed a competitiveness index, in which a perfectly competitive league would have a value of 1. The Premier League hasn't been anywhere near this since its first season.

Spanish counterparts. Between 2005/06 and 2008/09, the top four sides (who earned Champions League places) played the bottom three teams (who got relegated) a total of 96 times. In a mathematically competitive league, each team would win 13.67 games, giving the bottom three 41 victories. In a real-world competitive league, you would probably guesstimate that David would land one in Goliath's eye 15–20 times, even accounting for the differences that have, for now, put them at either end of the table. In fact the bottom three won just four of those 96 matches – an average of one between them per season. The top four sides won 78 of them, scoring 218 goals in the process – the bottom sides only kept five clean sheets, but failed far more often to score themselves, reaching a grand total of 49 goals. Reading's 3–1 home win over Liverpool in December 2007 was the only time any bottom-three side scored more than two goals in one of these encounters, and Rafael Benítez's decision to rest key players ahead of a Champions League trip to Marseille that would be quickly followed by the visit of Manchester United had as much to do with that as anything.

Even worse, the top four clubs at the end of each of those seasons were the same, the so-called Big Four of Arsenal, Chelsea, Liverpool and Manchester United forming an apparently impenetrable quadropoly. Such repetition was an unwanted first for English football. Though it isn't quite as grim as the Scottish Premier League (which hasn't been won by a team other than Celtic or Rangers since 1984), Norway's Tippeligaen, where Rosenborg won 14 consecutive titles between 1992 and 2004, or the Greek Super League, where Olympiacos and Panathinaikos have triumphed in 58 of its 84 seasons, it doesn't compare well with the other major European leagues. Italy, Spain, Germany, Holland and France have never had the same top four over a period of four seasons. You have to go to Portugal to find a league that exceeds England in this respect: a cartel of Belenenses, Benfica, Porto and Sporting Lisbon held sway for a whopping nine straight seasons, from 1951/52 to 1959/60.

The (top end of the) Premier League has become so utterly predictable that we have shifted our definition of excitement just to keep ourselves interested – we now celebrate a changing of the guard when a team breaks into the top *four*. Never mind actually challenging to win anything. While bookies rate Manchester United's chances of lifting the Premier League trophy in May 2012 at 11/10, Tottenham, who finished fifth in 2010/11, are at 150/1. Everton were considered easily capable of finishing seventh (at least before the loss of Mikel Arteta to Arsenal, just after the season started), but priced at more than 300/1 to win the league. It's rare for half the runners in the Grand National even to finish the race, yet you don't see odds like that. The last time a team came from outside the top four to push for the title the following season was in 1996/97, when Arsenal were four points off the top with two games to go, having finished fifth the year before (when actually they only missed out on fourth by three goals – they were level on points and goal difference with Aston Villa). Contrast that with the Bundesliga, where Borussia Dortmund actually won the title in 2011, having finished outside the top four for the previous seven seasons.

It takes hundreds of millions of pounds to smash the Premier League's glass ceiling. After increased investment in their squad, Tottenham Hotspur only missed fourth on a dramatic last day of the 2005/06 season, when a bout of food poisoning and a 2–1 reverse at West Ham left the players feeling a bit queasy. By the time they actually did break into the top four, in May 2010, they'd comprehensively outspent those above them – their financial results for the year ending June 2009 showed a transfer outlay of almost £150 million. The only club spending as much at the same time was Manchester City, who duly secured their Champions League spot by finishing third the following year. Only in the year after the owner Sheikh Mansour's investment in the club breached the £500 million mark, when Sergio Agüero and Samir Nasri arrived from Atlético Madrid and Arsenal respectively in the summer of 2011, did City start to be considered serious title contenders.

What used to be the Big Four is arguably, thanks to massive investment, becoming the Big Six, but excuse us if we don't string out the bunting just yet. Given that a proportion of Premier League income is distributed incrementally as you move up the table, the stagnation at the top has made the same few clubs richer and richer – a process that the booty of the Champions League (of which more later) has only made more devastating and dramatic. 'The top four, five, six teams are spending really highly and it's very difficult for us to compete,' said the Aston Villa manager Alex McLeish, in the summer of 2011. 'It is phenomenal. It's amazing the parameters that have now been set… you just can't compete.'

Between them the dominant cartel of credit card bullies have rarely even offered the compensatory thrill of dramatic denouements. The final day of the 1994/95 season was a bona fide classic, with Blackburn pipping Manchester United to the title despite losing at Liverpool, but only five out of 19 Premier League title races have gone to the final day – and only two of those to the final minute with one goal still in it (in 1995 and 1999). The last time a side won the title having started the day in second place was in 1989, with Arsenal's famous victory at Liverpool. Since then, such a switch has occurred four times in Spain (including three in a row), twice in Italy and three times in Germany.

In the first season of the Premier League, before the economic imbalance had taken hold, Norwich challenged for the title until the last month, and would have gone top with five games to play had they won at home to the eventual champions Manchester United rather than losing 3–1. In the end, Norwich finished third that year. What is remarkable is that the previous season they had finished 18th, avoiding relegation by three points – a margin narrow enough to convince at least one newspaper to tip them for relegation in 1992/93. The same was true of Graham Taylor's Aston Villa a few years previously (17th in 1988/89, second in 1989/90). You could even make the leap in the middle of the season. In 1981/82, Liverpool were 12th on New Year's Day yet stormed through the table to be champions. Derby did a similar thing in 1974/75, jumping from ninth at the turn of the year to first on the final day.

A competitive league is a gratifyingly fluid one. In 1983, Watford finished second – yet the league was so competitive (apart from the runaway leaders Liverpool) that they lost 15 of their 42 games. That was actually Watford's first season in the top flight; in the past, promoted sides could legitimately set their sights high. In 1977/78, Brian Clough's newly promoted Nottingham Forest won the title – the fifth such instance in English football, but surely the last for a long time. It is beyond improbable that a freshly promoted side could be crowned champions in today's Premier League; instead their ambitions are generally limited to finishing 17th, and thus avoiding relegation. In 19 seasons of Premier League football, 26 of 56 promoted sides have been relegated in their first season, with another eight succumbing to the Grim Reaper of football: second-season syndrome. The 2001/02 season is notable for being the only time that all three newly promoted teams – Fulham, Blackburn Rovers and Bolton Wanderers – survived. Shockingly, Saturday September 17th 2011 was notable because it was the first time in four-and-a-half-years that all three promoted clubs had actually won on the same day. At the bottom, at least, the Premier League remains livelier than Luton High Street on a Saturday night, only with slightly less dignity come chucking-out time.

Part of the problem, of course, is that the best players in the league end up at the same few clubs, sooner or later. Though it was primarily designed with the interests of young home-grown players in mind, it was envisaged that the 25-man squad limit introduced by the Premier League ahead of the 2010/11 season would prevent the biggest clubs hoarding talent, because they would only be able to field the players named at the start of the season, and only 17 of those named could be foreign players older than 21. But its effect in this regard is undermined completely by the loan system, which allows them to continue buying anyone they spot playing a pass with the outside of his boot – lest he should actually end up being good enough to be a nuisance to them from elsewhere – and then lending them to other clubs. In the case of younger players, they're often shipped out to the lower leagues, from where they can do no harm to their parent club (31-year-old Craig Bellamy's loan move from Manchester City to League One Cardiff in 2010 for the same reasons being a notable and frankly immoral irregularity). Many others are farmed out to fellow Premier League clubs, where they are contractually obliged to sit out the two fixtures against their parent club. 'I don't believe clubs stockpile players,' said chief executive Richard Scudamore, when asked if the Premier League might do anything about the trend, in September 2009. 'It's not in their interests.' Right-o.

If you look at England's 2010 World Cup squad, you'll see that 20 of Fabio Capello's 23-man squad came from the teams who had finished in the top seven the previous season (including, by the by, Joe Hart, bought by Manchester City for £600,000 from Shrewsbury Town in May 2006 and loaned out to League One sides Tranmere Rovers and Blackpool before getting a run of games at City. The goalkeeper also went on loan to Birmingham City for the 2009/10 season after Shay Given arrived from Newcastle United and moved straight into the No. 1 spot – when Birmingham travelled to Eastlands in the final weeks of that season with Maik Taylor making his first appearance for five months, in Hart's stead, they were absolutely destroyed, conceding five). England's squad at the 2006 World Cup also featured 20 top-seven players; in 2002 it was 18; in 1998, 15 out of 22; and in 1990, it was just 7 out of 22.

The PFA Team of the Year offers further evidence in this regard. Between 2008 and 2011 it comprised players from only five teams, a far cry from the 1981/82 team, which included players from nine teams: Peter Shilton (Nottingham Forest), Kenny Swain (Aston Villa), David O'Leary (Arsenal), Alan Hansen (Liverpool), Kenny Sansom (Arsenal), Graeme Souness (Liverpool), Glenn Hoddle (Tottenham Hotspur), Bryan Robson (Manchester United), Trevor Francis (Manchester City), Kevin Keegan (Southampton) and Cyrille Regis (West Bromwich Albion).

It is impossible to imagine a contemporary repeat, because

the premise of the Premier League is precisely that the biggest clubs should thrive at the expense of others. There are simple, if not entirely straightforward, ways to address today's disparities, yet nobody will even consider things like salary caps, or some kind of draft system. They might sound outlandish, but then so did the back-pass law, and in this instance the reluctance is not conservatism, it's contempt. Advocating a free-market approach as early as 1985, the then Manchester United chairman Martin Edwards said that: 'The smaller clubs are bleeding the game dry. For the sake of the game, they should be put to sleep.' The threat from 'smaller clubs' has been successfully mitigated, if not euthanised, but it has been rather more for the sake of profit than the game.

A GREAT ADVERT FOR CRICKET: THE FA CUP

There is no beer belly in the world more beautiful than Dave Radford's. It may lack the power that makes Tony Soprano's seem so desirable, or the humour that does the same for someone such as Jack Black, but it is a symbol of something even greater. The reason for Radford's beer belly is that every time he meets someone new they want to buy him a drink; the reason for that is that he is the brother of Ronnie, whose astonishing long-range screamer for Hereford against Newcastle in 1972 is the magic of the FA Cup *in excelsis*.

There is so much to enjoy about the chronicle of this encounter, even down to the five postponements wrought by the weather – when Edgar Street finally hosted Newcastle for the replay, the pitch was still indistinguishable from a bog. Ronnie Radford was a part-time carpenter, playing for a non-league side who considered it a good week if they trained together once. Newcastle boasted the likes of England striker Malcolm Macdonald, player of the season Tony Green and fans' favourite John Tudor (still considered by some to be the best player ever to pull on a Newcastle shirt); they weren't exactly taking the First Division by storm, but not since Yeovil Town had beaten Sunderland in 1949 had a team from as far down the food chain as Hereford won a competitive match against a top-flight club.

Macdonald, who thought he'd scored the winner with eight minutes to go, insisted that Radford's equaliser was fortunate – 'the ball sat up on a divot… it would've been a mishit and a throw-in to us' – but it was a phenomenal shot, regardless, hit from outside of the box after a galloping one-two with Brian Owen. The crowd didn't pause to worry about divots as they poured on to the pitch, led from the front by the policemen on duty. 'When Ronnie scored the crowd ran on, but I was ahead of them, cheering,' remembered one local bobby, Grenville Smith. 'I threw my police hat in the air, caught it, then remembered myself and shouted: "Off the pitch!"'

Those of a certain age were brought up on the regular repeats of this goal, which is as deliciously evocative of childhood as the opening credits to *Napoleon Dynamite* or a freshly rediscovered schoolbook. It is something you can view again and again and still feel the spine shiver and the hairs on the back of the neck do a little dance, an unashamed feel-good classic: the goal itself, the pitch invasion, and finally Radford's grandad-who-has-just-won-the-lottery-and-whose-knees-are-going-to-go-any-second-now celebration trot.

What a shame that modern football seems so utterly incapable of producing a moment of such homespun charm, human spirit and humble joy. Nostalgia sometimes lends these things a helping hand – you know you're in a different era when you find that Hereford defender Roger Griffiths played most of the match on a broken leg – but the FA Cup used to be guaranteed to produce some of the season's most colourful moments, not just rose-tinted ones. Open to all and sundry, meetings between clubs whose paths would never usually cross captured everyone's imagination, and the final – always the final day of the season – was like Christmas. 'Cup final day used to be the day of the year when I was growing up,' said Harry Redknapp, who led Portsmouth to the trophy in 2008. 'The streets were empty, everybody was watching, it was the thing.'

Few developments in modern football have provoked such undiluted sadness as the demise of the FA Cup. If the spirit of English football could be encapsulated in one thing, it would be the FA Cup: a chance for anyone in the pyramid to have a go and see how fate was feeling. It mattered. 'The FA Cup final is the greatest single match outside the World Cup final,' Sir Bobby Robson once said, and time was you'd have been hard pushed to argue. In recent years, however, the FA Cup has lost so much of its lustre that it's almost impossible to see how it can regain its former status.

In truth, the FA hasn't always helped matters, increasingly happy for its showpiece to defer to questionable demands. The decision to allow Spurs and Arsenal to play their 1991 FA Cup semi-final at Wembley was taken because it was felt that no neutral venue could properly accommodate the tie, but it stripped the final of its unique glamour. In the following years the FA appeared to wrestle with its conscience, playing both semi-finals at Wembley in 1993 (the north London sides met again) and 1994, before switching back to neutral grounds – except for the 2000 semi-finals, which went back to the soon-to-be-demolished Wembley. Once the new stadium was under construction and over budget, the FA announced that all semi-finals would be held there once it was open; once-in-a-lifetime trips don't pay the bills.

The FA has so far shown itself to be immune to supporters' distaste at the watering down of a Wembley awayday (or the lunacy of forcing four teams down to London from the north, as happened in 2011), but it can be incredibly obliging, allowing Arsenal to play their Champions League 'home' games at Wembley in 1998 and 1999 so that UEFA's oversized advertising hoardings didn't eat into capacity (playing at Wembley virtually doubled it). The cup itself suffered a symbolic blow in 1999/2000, when the FA pressured Manchester United into pulling out of the competition so that they could play, at the invitation of FIFA, in the inaugural World Club Championship in Brazil. The plan was to butter up Sepp and Co. while they were considering hosts for the 2006 World Cup, but this backfired spectacularly as Blatter later announced that the competition would have no impact on the bidding process. Germany, who didn't send a team, got the gig.

Perhaps the biggest insult to the FA Cup's traditions, however, was the decision to play the 2011 final alongside league fixtures. The FA had signed a contract with UEFA agreeing not to host any events on the Wembley pitch less than two weeks prior to the Champions League final booked in for May 28th. That these two weeks covered what should have been final day didn't seem to make any difference. To make matters worse, the league games on that day included the title decider between Blackburn Rovers and Manchester United, which kicked off early. Stoke and Manchester City, in their first final for decades, were demoted to a sideshow with City forced to celebrate victory in the shadow of United winning their record-breaking 19th League title.

Ultimately, however, the FA Cup is an unfortunate victim in a world where everything has a price and nothing a value. On winning the trophy in 2011, City were given a cheque for £1.8 million – about what it costs them to keep Yaya Touré, scorer of the winning goal, for two months. On this occasion they were glad of the silverware, their first trophy for 35 years heralding the start of a new and successful era, but that attitude is likely to prove as anomalous for City as it is for the FA Cup. The money involved in the Premier League and the Champions League so dwarfs FA Cup payouts that it is left a distant third in terms of priorities – most teams would rather finish fourth and qualify for the Champions League, or finish 17th and cling to their Premier League status, than win the FA Cup.

As a result, what became a few years ago common practice in the League Cup – fielding reserve sides until you got close enough to the final to bother naming your first team – has increasingly been adopted in the FA Cup. In March 2011 the Aston Villa manager Gérard Houllier upset fans by excusing the influential trio of Ashley Young, Stewart Downing and Marc Albrighton from duty for their fifth-round meeting with Manchester City, saying he wanted to rest them for a match against Bolton Wanderers three days later – at this point Villa sat mid-table, but with teams jostling within a point or two of one another, he felt his team were vulnerable. This might not have been so galling for Villa supporters had a team featuring those three not beaten City six weeks earlier, making a quarter-final appearance feasible (even having had to swap the cup-tied Darren Bent for Emile Heskey), and had they not then lost to Bolton anyway. Speaking in Houllier's defence, the Liverpool manager Kenny Dalglish wrote in the *Daily Mail*: 'I am trying to be rational and say what Villa did at City on Wednesday night is going to be repeated by many clubs over the years unless something can be done at the top of the game to make the FA Cup special again.' It was a sentiment that the Queens Park Rangers manager Neil Warnock echoed after his side exited the 2011/12 League Cup with defeat to Rochdale in the second round: 'I don't think people care about the competition… they should revamp the cup.' Neither seemed to think that managers' attitudes – Warnock said he was 'not disappointed to be out; the competition is not a priority for us'– might have a part to play in restoring a bit of the competitions' old sparkle.

Weakened teams serve to place an asterisk against shocks when they do happen. In the past, when a lower-league or non-league side slew a giant, they knew they had beaten the best their opponents had to offer. Billy Bremner was missing through injury when Leeds United – top of the First Division and flying under Don Revie – were beaten by Fourth Division Colchester United in the fifth round in 1971, but Peter Lorimer said: 'It was so embarrassing for everybody. It wasn't that we had a weakened side, we had a good side.' These days, it's more like David slaying Goliath while Goliath had a dicky knee and a dodgy tummy.

Despite that, the chances of an upset have become increasingly minuscule. Such is the economic imbalance in modern football that a second-string from the biggest clubs can usually fend off the full-strength challenge of even Championship sides. The underdog story is now almost exclusively one of valiant defeat, and the noble draw against a heavily weakened Premier League side is the new giant-killing. As charming as such stories still are, they don't drip with anywhere near as much romance as the likes of Hereford in 1972 or Sutton, who were the last non-league team to beat top-flight opposition when they toppled Coventry City in 1989. Despite being a knockout competition, the FA Cup is about as competitive as the Premier League: since 1992/93, seven different teams have won it, with Arsenal, Chelsea, Liverpool or Manchester United winning 16 out of 19 finals, six of which were contested by two of the four. In the previous two decades there had been 11 winners. In the two decades before that, there were 17 different names inscribed on the cup. The last shock of even minor proportions in an FA Cup final was probably Everton's win over United in 1995; for the last major shock you have to go back to 1988, when Wimbledon beat Liverpool.

Accustomed to victory, the big clubs have become indifferent to it. Manchester United won the FA Cup in 2004, Arsenal in 2005 and Chelsea in 2007, yet all three seasons ultimately went down as disappointments because the clubs failed to retain the League title. The FA Cup has become supplementary, a trinket to add extra glitter to a good season as part of a double or treble. Yet such is the dominance of these few clubs in recent years that even doubles have lost their shine – after five doubles in the first 106 years of English football, there have been six in the last 17 years. The manager Carlo Ancelotti was sacked within 12 months of winning Chelsea's first-ever Premier League and FA Cup double in 2009/10.

Preparing for the 1948 final, the Manchester United forward Stan Pearson was constantly thinking of a simple motivational sentence from his manager, Sir Matt Busby: 'The greatest thrill in soccer is playing at Wembley on Cup Final day.' United hadn't won the trophy since 1909 (there had been 23 different winners in the intervening 28 finals – two world wars having disrupted the competition), and beat Blackpool 4–2 in an immense match described by the attending press as 'one of the greatest cup finals in history'. It doesn't bear comparison to any recent FA Cup finals, the best of which was the deranged 3–3 draw between Liverpool and West Ham in 2006. Too often sides are so used to playing in the FA Cup final that they go about them with all the enthusiasm of a man doing his tax return, and only because his wife will make him re-tile the bathroom if he doesn't – describing the 2007 final between Chelsea and Manchester United, BBC commentator Mark Lawrenson said it was 'a great advert for cricket'.

While the final – once an impossibly glamorous festival and the most important day in the English football calendar – is the outstanding symbol of the FA Cup's demise, it is not the only one. The tournament as a whole suffers the trampling of tradition and the poverty of imagination shown by leading managers. Some of the things that made the FA Cup special are gone, and there is no getting them back: now that live matches make for everyday television, the fizz in the pit of your stomach at catching sight of a team coach pulling into Wembley, or a team captain introducing his teammates, has been snuffed. As Chapter Five discusses, there are very good reasons why football fans would be loath to give up their Sky Sports subscription, no matter how much they loathe Ray Wilkins' yadda-yadda-yadda. But we might be permitted to miss sticking our ear to the radio to hear the draw for the next round on a Monday lunchtime (even the random celebrities called in to do the TV draw on a Sunday don't seem to know why they, or Jim Rosenthal, are there. The day that That One Out Of Kasabian did it was a spectacular nadir.) Or the classic, never-ending replay marathons (think 1979, when Arsenal and Sheffield Wednesday played five times in under three weeks to settle a third-round tie) that have been scuppered by the introduction of penalty shootouts. Or simply the days when no manager had to 'prioritise' to the extent that the 'greatest thrill in soccer' becomes a chore.

HAEMORRHAGING GRANDEUR AND GRAVITAS: EUROPEAN LEAGUES

Il campionato più bello del mondo. The most beautiful championship in the world. That's what the Italians proudly called Serie A for much of the 1980s and almost all of the 1990s. And so it was. For those of a certain age, the intrinsic superiority of Serie A was as much of a given as the Pope's religion and the location of Yogi Bear's toilet.

All that changed on April 21st 1999. When Manchester United came back from 2–0 down to beat Juventus 3–2 in the Champions League semi-final, many in England thought it was the beginning of an era of United dominance. It turned out to be no such thing. But it was certainly the end of an era: no Italian side had lost a European Cup knockout game at home for an incredible 20 years. Juventus had outplayed United to a startling degree while drawing 1–1 at Old Trafford, and eased into a 2–0 lead in the first 11 minutes of the return. Then Roy Keane entered a zone of chilling certainty, and the coolly emphatic manner in which United went through – they should have won by more, hitting the post twice – thrust a stunned Serie A into a prolonged period of introspection. What should logically have been a one-off result, easy to write off, instead led to a staggering slump in the efficacy of Italian football. There hasn't been such a striking difference between before and after since Barry Bethell went on the Slim-Fast Plan.

The best way to measure the health of a league is in international competition: in that respect, Serie A has not recovered from that grisly night in Turin. In 2000 the UEFA coefficients painted an impressive picture of Italian football: Juventus were the top-ranked team, and the top ten boasted four Italian sides (Manchester United were sixth); overall Serie A was second to Spain's La Liga, but together they were head, shoulders and torso above Germany, France and England, who were bunched from third to fifth in that order. We wouldn't rely on stats to tell the whole picture (the Association of Football Statisticians' Top 100 Footballers list, released in 2007, omitted George Best and 1966 England captain Bobby Moore but included the very good, but hardly comparable, Jon Dahl Tomasson and Gary Neville), but the time lag – they are based on the previous five years' results in European competition – if nothing else makes them fairly useful. By 2005, Juventus had dropped out of the top ten – as had Lazio and Parma; only Internazionale remained, with AC Milan having risen to join them. Manchester United remained in sixth, although the Premier League now boasted a second and third representative with Liverpool and Arsenal occupying fifth and tenth spots respectively. Serie A had been overhauled by the Premier League and was now barely able to see La Liga for dust.

If Serie A's downward spiral began in 1999, it was accelerated in 2006 when investigators found evidence that linked a number of club officials to refereeing organisations, implicating Juventus, Milan, Lazio, Fiorentina and Reggina in a match-fixing scandal. After a summer of claim and counter-claim, punishment and appeal, Juventus were stripped of their last two Serie A titles, relegated to Serie B and booted out of the Champions League, as were Fiorentina. Milan were allowed back into European competition on appeal, but Serie A itself had taken a serious hit.

	2005/06	2006/07	2007/08	2008/09	2009/10	2010/11
England	14.428	16.625	**17.875**	**15.000**	17.928	**18.357**
Spain	**15.642**	**19.000**	13.875	13.312	17.928	18.214
Germany	10.437	9.500	13.500	12.687	**18.083**	15.666
Italy	15.357	11.928	10.250	11.375	15.428	11.571

The table above shows the UEFA co-efficients (based on each country's clubs' results in that season's Champions and Europa League competitions) for England, Spain, Germany and Italy between 2006 and 2011. We're not always that dazzled by numbers, and there are a few in UEFA's stats that urge caution – the fact that Romania was actually the highest-ranking country in 2005/06, on the basis that Steaua and Rapid Bucharest made the latter stages of the UEFA Cup, for a start (which is why rankings are worked out on a five-year aggregate score). But it's worth noting that the Italians have been outscored by Germany's Bundesliga in every season since 2007/08, even with the bounce that Internazionale's Champions League victory gave Serie A's stats in 2009/10; Inter's victory and AC Milan's Champions League wins in 2003 and 2007 were isolated triumphs, in no way reflecting a period of dominance such as that enjoyed in previous decades. Serie A had nine European Cup/Champions League finalists in the ten seasons from 1988 to 1998; from 1999 to 2011 they had just five in 13. By the 2011/12 season Serie A had slipped to fourth in the overall country rankings, having scored lower for the 2010/11 season than sixth-placed Portugal and only marginally better than the Netherlands, France, Russia and Ukraine. Milan and Internazionale clung to the bottom two positions in the club top ten, with Sevilla, Werder Bremen and Olympique Lyonnais all jockeying for position close behind.

How the mighty have fallen. A domestic league has surely never been as superior as Serie A in the late 1980s and 1990s. It was so seductively chic and suffused with importance that the world's best players were drawn to Italy like VIPs to the coolest after-party. The highlights reel from 1990/91, for example, would feature some truly memorable strikes from the likes of Roberto Mancini, Alessandro Melli, Diego Simeone, Jürgen Klinsmann and Gianluca Vialli (and this in a season when almost a third of all matches brought a maximum of one goal). Goals may have been at a premium but the entertainment was generally of a subtler kind. Serie A wowed its disciples with displays of an intimidating high technical and tactical quality.

The whole business was so otherworldly, and conducted with such operatic intensity, that you felt it should have been played out on the stage of La Scala rather than the pitch of the San Siro. In Italy, *calcio* was consumed with a passion that made religion seem almost frivolous by comparison. Serie A gave off an intoxicating pheromonal musk, never more so than in a title decider between Internazionale and Sampdoria in May 1991, for which the word 'epic' feels flimsy and inadequate. The equation was simple: Inter needed to win, Sampdoria not to lose. What unfolded was unimaginable. Sampdoria won 2–0 but could feasibly have lost 10–4. The Sky commentator Martin Tyler, a calm, gentle man not given to hyperbole (at least when he's not growling 'IT'S LIVE!' before a Sky match these days), had lost it completely by the end of the game, announcing that 'In years to come, people will be saying,"I was here. I was at that game"… Grown men, hardened football-watchers, are scarcely able to turn their eyes to this.'

Since then, however, the grandeur and gravitas have haemorrhaged from Serie A, leaving it weedy and anaemic. 'We are on the second level now,' said Fabio Licari of the *Gazzetta dello Sport* in 2008.'England and Spain represent the top level, and Italy are now with Germany and France on the second level.' In England, Serie A enjoys nothing like the reverence it used to. English teams have beaten Italian opposition easily in Europe in the last decade. In 2003/04, Arsenal won 5–1 at Inter and Chelsea 4–0 at Lazio. In 2006/07, Manchester United beat Roma 7–1; three seasons later they eviscerated AC Milan 7–2 on aggregate. In the mid-90s, however, English clubs travelled to Italy with little more than a passport and a prayer. The current state of affairs is as incongruous as HBO making tacky soaps or Radiohead releasing throwaway pop. The whole *point* of Serie A was that it was the best; otherwise the fervour seems vaguely ludicrous. Just as cricket needs a strong West Indies, rugby a strong New Zealand, so football needs a strong Serie A.

Back in the day, Italy almost had a monopoly on the world's best talent. Between 1982 and 1998, 13 of the 17 Ballon d'Or winners were playing in Italy at the time: Paolo Rossi, Michel Platini (three times), Roberto Baggio and

Zinedine Zidane at Juventus; Ruud Gullit, Marco van Basten (three times) and George Weah at Milan; and Lothar Matthäus and Ronaldo for Internazionale. In 1995, Serie A provided 11 of the top 20 players on the Ballon d'Or shortlist, with Weah winning ahead of Alessandro Del Piero, Fabrizio Ravanelli, Paulo Sousa and Gianluca Vialli (Juve), Gianfranco Zola and Hristo Stoichkov (Parma), Paolo Maldini, Marcel Desailly and Dejan Savićević (Milan), and Gabriel Batistuta (Fiorentina). Five years earlier, when Italian club football was arguably at its apex, they had seven of the top nine. Matthäus was picked by 25 of the 29 voters, and that year he became the ninth Serie A player in a row to be named *World Soccer* Player of the Year.

Since then, they have had just three winners (for pub quizzers: Pavel Nedved in 2003, Andriy Shevchenko in 2004 and Kaká in 2007). In 2010, only four of the 23 men shortlisted for the Ballon d'Or played in Italy, and that was on account of the unprecedented treble won in José Mourinho's second (and last) year in charge of Internazionale; the spine of that team, from Júlio César in goal to Samuel Eto'o up front, via Maicon and Wesley Sneijder, was nominated. A year earlier, Eto'o had been the only man from the Serie A in the top 20.

The best players now invariably end up in Spain or England, from where 15 of the last 26 Champions League finalists have come (they had collectively provided three finalists between 1988 and 1998, which makes this shift all the more remarkable.) Not even in the six finals between 1989 and 1994, when AC Milan won three titles, have two countries squeezed out all others so effectively. Serie A's credibility was damaged enormously in the summers of 2001 and 2002, when Real Madrid bought Zinedine Zidane and

Since the introduction of three points for a win and 38 games in 1997/98, the points total of the Spanish champions has risen considerably: 74, 79, 69, 80, 75, 78, 77, 84, 82, 76, 85, 87, 99, 96. In 2009/10, when Barcelona took the title with 99 points, the clubs managed an astonishing 195 points between them, as Real Madrid finished second with 96. Second! Having lost just four games! It's hard to find an equivalent in the history of world football. Reading and Sheffield United shared 196 points in the Championship in 2005/06 – but that came over 46 games in a 24-team league rather than the 38 games and 20-team league that is the Spanish top flight. Rangers (85) and Celtic (103) combined for 188 points in the Scottish Premier League in 2001/02. Barry Town's 104-point romp to the Welsh title in 1997/98, when combined with runners-up Newtown, adds up to 182. Italy's best is 172 in 2006/07.

It was not always thus. In the last 40 years of La Liga, there have been a couple of distinct cycles in which other sides have emerged: between 1981 and 1984, when first Real Sociedad and then Athletic Bilbao won back-to-back titles, and from 1999 to 2004, when three of the five titles were claimed by Deportivo La Coruña and Valencia. Valencia also reached consecutive Champions League finals in 2000 and 2001. Since Valencia won the title in 2003/04, no outsider has finished in the top two apart from Villarreal, who came second in 2007/08. Before that it happened eight times out of ten – Real and Barcelona did not even monopolise the top three: of the 11 seasons between 1993 and 2004, Real and Barcelona only finished in the top three together on two occasions, in 1994/95 and 1996/97.

In 2000, Real finished as low as fifth; three years later, Barcelona finished sixth. At that stage, La Liga was an object lesson in how to combine competitiveness with real quality. Not only were the best teams often beaten, they were occasionally trounced in a way that did not happen anywhere near as often in England or Italy. It was particularly the case with Barcelona, who seemed to be genetically predisposed to the occasional epic shocker. The list reads like a David and Goliath-on. They lost 6–3 at Zaragoza in 1993/94, 5–0 at Racing Santander in 1994/95, 4–0 at Tenerife in 1996/97, 4–1 at home to Salamanca and 5–2 at Atlético Madrid in 1997/98, 4–0 at Santander in 2000/01, and 5–1 at Malaga in 2003/04. Real Madrid didn't escape eithcr. They were thrashed 4–0 at home to Osasuna in 1990/91, 4–0 at Deportivo in 1993/94, 4–0 at Celta Vigo in 1996/97, 5–1 at Celta and 4–0 at Deportivo in 1998/99, 5–2 at Deportivo and 5–1 at home to Real Zaragoza in 1999/2000, 5–1 at home to Mallorca in 2002/03, 3–0 at home to Osasuna and 4–1 at home to Real Sociedad in 2003/04.

These sorts of results date their occasions as readily as David Beckham haircuts. In the last two seasons, Barcelona have lost three games – they lost more than that in a month during the 1999/2000 season. The 2003/04 season was the last in which Barcelona conceded five goals in a league match, and the 2002/03 campaign was the last in which Real conceded five or more to anyone other than Barcelona.

A similar story has long since emerged in La Liga's spiritual sibling, the Scottish Premier League. Rangers and Celtic have won the last 26 titles between them; the last time a non-Old Firm side finished within even ten points of the title was in 1997/98, when Hearts might have caught Rangers but for a late run of draws. At least they had the consolation of beating them in the Scottish Cup. Hearts are also the last team to break into the top two: in 2005/06, the only instance since 1995. The gap between the top two and the rest is so big that not even the maddest stuntman would try jumping it. In 2001/02, Celtic finished a preposterous 45 points ahead of third-placed Livingstone.

For nostalgics, the biggest problem in Scottish football is not the lack of competitiveness, however, but the dramatic drop in quality. This will be hard for younger readers to comprehend but, not that long ago, Scottish football was *brilliant*, an incomparable cocktail of mischief, anarchy, flair and booze. It was football as nature intended. If one moment sums up Scottish football as was, it is Hearts' winning goal at Rangers in December 1972, when Tommy Murray goaded the Rangers players and Ibrox fans by sitting on the ball in the build-up to Donald Ford's decisive header. You didn't need a degree in swearing to imagine the patter in the Rangers end as that went in.

Murray's sit-down was a riposte to a similar stunt pulled by Rangers' own Willie Johnston against Hearts. Johnston was one of a phalanx of brilliant, maverick wingers – many truly blessed with genius – that Scotland produced in the 1970s and 1980s: Jimmy Johnstone, Charlie Cooke, Davie Cooper, John Robertson, Eddie Gray, Pat Nevin, Ralph Milne. Never mind whistling down a mine; in Scotland you had to whistle down a pub and you would find a player. It is incredible to think that, when Celtic's Lisbon Lions became the first British side to win the European Cup in 1967, their team was comprised entirely of players born within 30 miles of Glasgow.

There are few such talents now, and of Scotland's squad for the Euro 2012 qualifiers against the Czech Republic and Lithuania, only five played their club football in Scotland – exclusively for Celtic or Rangers. For the most part, Scottish football is an afterthought to those outside Scotland. There have been occasional stirrings in Europe – Celtic and Rangers reached the UEFA Cup finals of 2004 and 2008 respectively – yet there has been no such success in the Champions League. Since Rangers came within one goal of reaching the final in 1992/93, the best a Scottish side has done is to reach the last 16. In the 2011/12 season, all three Scottish clubs had been put out of European competition by the end of August – although the removal of the Swiss outfit FC Sion, for fielding ineligible players, gave Celtic another chance to be humiliated in the Europa League.

Throughout the 2000s, the big idea for redressing the balance in the SPL has been for Rangers and Celtic to jump ship and join the English top flight, giving them a share of the Big Fat Premier League Pot and leaving the rest of the Scottish league to rot play amongst themselves. 'Celtic and Rangers have outgrown the SPL,' harrumphed Terry Butcher, not long after his Motherwell side had had their backsides handed to them by Celtic in 2005. 'I hope the Old Firm clear off and give the rest of us a chance.' Perhaps not surprisingly, governing bodies have not so far been moved to interrogate the faintly ludicrous idea that any club is able naturally to 'outgrow' a league without the distorting influence of considerable amounts of money. In Scotland, Celtic and Rangers have been cast as unlucky, trapped in a league that's beneath them; the uncertainty of the Scottish league's earning potential without them facetiously plays into that idea. And it's precisely the same fear that gives Real Madrid and Barcelona leverage when their dominance – which is now so excessive that Sevilla President José María Del Nido labelled La Liga 'the greatest pile of junk in Europe' – comes up for debate in Spain. Responding to Del Nido, Madrid defender Sergio Ramos said: 'If he doesn't like it, he can find himself another league.'

ANOTHER FINE MESS: EUROPEAN COMPETITION

When Manchester United won the Premier League title on May 6th 2007, Sir Alex Ferguson settled down in front of the camera for the usual celebratory interview. It was a vital triumph for Ferguson, one of his most cathartic: his first championship for four years, and a decisive rejoinder to the severe criticism he had received in the media 18 months earlier. Ferguson, his genius reasserted, wore the broadest of smiles as he supped champagne and talked. Then the interviewer asked him about United's defeat to AC Milan in the European Cup semi-final four days earlier. Ferguson's eyes glazed over, and suddenly he wore the crestfallen expression of a newly heartbroken man staring absent-mindedly at a shelf of spirits. For about 20 seconds, all he could think about was the one that got away.

Some 47 years earlier, on May 18th 1960, the 18-year-old Alex Ferguson stood in the schoolboys' enclosure at Hampden Park, in Glasgow, to watch Real Madrid play Eintracht Frankfurt in the fifth European Cup final. The match finished 7–3 to Real Madrid. Alfredo Di Stéfano became one of only three men in the history of the competition to score a hat-trick in the final. His fellow striker that day was Hungary's Ferenc Puskás. He scored four. 'The thousands of people at the game must have thought that they were dreaming,' said the report in the following morning's *Daily Mail*. Ferguson wasn't the only one smitten for life by this experience of football beyond its normal dimensions.

European competition was football at its most exotic, glamorous, mysterious and seductive.

The old system was almost perfect. The European Cup was the big one, the UEFA Cup was a kind of alternative prom, and just about the only thing wrong with the Cup Winners' Cup was the fact that nobody knew where to put the apostrophe, or whether there needed to be one in the first place. In recent years, however, UEFA have managed to make such a sorry mess of things that European football is a shadow of what it was. The Cup Winners' Cup has gone, the UEFA Cup has been horribly compromised and the European Cup desecrated. If you haven't spotted the theme yet, this has all been done in the pursuit of greater and greater revenue, naked commercialism having latterly transformed the last 16 (where did 'round of 16' come from?) from a single night of unadulterated *Sports Report* geekery-overload into a month-long money-spinning television marathon, and obliterated 55 years of tradition with the move to Saturday-night Champions League finals.

Going by the familiar maxim, if it ain't broke, slap it about a bit until some coins fall out, UEFA introduced a group stage in place of the quarter- and semi-finals in 1991/92. This would guarantee the big sides a certain number of games, and thus a certain level of revenue, per season, provided they could successfully negotiate the theoretically easy early rounds. The tournament was then renamed the Champions League in 1993, with the same structure. A year later they restored the semi-finals but kept the group stage, then in 1994 they moved the group stages back – so that automatic qualifiers would be guaranteed six games, with the top two in each group going through to the quarter-finals. The group stage is totally against the spirit of the European Cup as it was first conceived.[9] It had been an unseeded knockout competition, which imbued the pre-Christmas matches with all sorts of drama – one false move, and you were done for. You could wait a decade to play in the European Cup and be out by the end of September. As Internazionale were in 1989/90.

The most damaging compromise, however, was still to come. In 1997, the tournament expanded, with some domestic runners-up allowed in. By 1999, as many as four teams from Europe's premier leagues were allowed in, as UEFA attempted to quash the threat of a breakaway competition by giving clubs the extra revenue they wanted. Before that, to reach the European Cup you had to either win your league or the European Cup itself. Since the also-rans were allowed in, only one final has been between two sides that won their domestic title the previous season: Real Madrid 1–0 Juventus in 1998. In the 21st century, the Champions League dukes it out with America's World Series of baseball to see which is the sporting world's biggest and most delusional misnomer.

Thanks to its frantic materialism, the competition as it is suffers another 21st-century, first-world problem: obesity. It is

---

[9] We confess to being excited by some group matches at first, partly because they were novel, and particularly because the competition retained a cut-throat edge. In 1998/99, there was one of the great Groups of Death: Barcelona, Bayern Munich, Manchester United and Brondby, with only one guaranteed qualifier (there were six groups, with the winners and the top two second-placed teams going through). It was a classic, with 44 goals in 12 games. In the end United and Bayern both got through and went all the way to the final. A year later, Barcelona were involved in another classic group, with Arsenal and the Italian dark horses Fiorentina. By now two sides were guaranteed qualification, but it still meant one had to go early. Gabriel Batistuta's unforgettable thunderbolt put Arsenal out.

now a lumbering, mouth-breathing beast. In 1990/91, the last tournament played before the competition was expanded, there were 59 games. In 2010/11, there were 125 – and that's not including the qualifying rounds, which start almost a year before the final; in total, there were 213 matches. In a sense – and this is the Champions League's boast – the admission of more teams from the continent's best leagues and the round-robin element make the trophy harder to win than the old European Cup. Nobody has retained the Champions League; the last club to do so in the European Cup was AC Milan in 1990. Yet part of the perception is misguided. People look at the routes taken to win the competition in the 1970s and 1980s and sneer at the low quality of the opposition, but that is to judge them by present-day standards rather than in their own time; sides like Dinamo Bucharest and Górnik Zabrze used to be seriously hard work.

Besides, in the beginning seeding kept the biggest clubs apart for one round. Now they have a six-game group stage to find their rhythm, providing the lucky spectator with 96 matches that Paul the Octopus's desperately thick brother Cecil could correctly predict. They're close to a formality for the biggest clubs, who have become so accustomed to qualifying from the group that the last-16 stage is the first point at which they feel even remotely vulnerable – in fact after a spate of 'early' exits for Barcelona, Manchester United, Real Madrid and Arsenal in the first half of the 2000s, United chief executive David Gill actually suggested that UEFA seed the last 16 in order to protect certain clubs. 'At the moment we effectively have a random draw after the group stage,' he huffed. What do UEFA think this is? A knockout competition?

To soften the blow of missing out on qualification from the

group stages, UEFA now transports the third-placed losers directly into the UEFA Cup/Europa League at the third-round stage. The impact of the change – made alongside the decision to permit more clubs to compete in the Champions League – has been to almost fatally weaken the Europa League, which must suffer clubs (who would by the old rules have qualified 'only' for the UEFA Cup in any case, if they qualified for anything at all) turning up halfway through and bitching about what a bad time they're having. In 1999, when Arsenal's defeat to Fiorentina gave them an early opportunity to try the new parachute, Ray Parlour moaned: 'It is a load of rubbish playing in the UEFA Cup.'

Perceiving it as the booby prize for Champions League failures, many teams now treat the Europa League with utter disdain. In 2011, Bayern Munich midfielder Arjen Robben told German newspaper *Bild*, in all seriousness: 'That is the worst that can happen. I think it is better if you don't play at all. Even winning the Europa League would not mean anything for me… it is not something I want.' Robben was speaking at a time when Bayern looked in danger of finishing the season outside of the Bundesliga Champions League places; in the end they finished third. If you're happy to play in the Champions League on the basis of being the third-best team in Germany, it seems daft in the extreme that you should get so sniffy about mixing it in the Europa League. Robben's attitude is shared by deluded fans across the continent, and their fetishising of an elite, often trophy-less, but always well-paid status is not only anathema to the spirit of football, it's a plain shame, because the tournament has, in spite of everything, retained a degree of innocence and charm. It is frequently populated by teams who do not perceive European football as their birthright, and thus still have the child-like enthusiasm of old. One of the most exhilarating matches anywhere in the last few years came at Goodison Park, when Fiorentina arrived for the second leg of their fourth-round tie armed with a two-goal lead. Everton levelled the scores but lost on penalties on a night so marvellously ingenuous and naked and unsanitised on and off the field that it reminded you why you fell in love with football in the first place. Further north, Middlesbrough fans will forever talk about their two four-goal comebacks in the quarter- and semi-finals of 2005/06. So will Steve McClaren. Without them, he would not have got the England job.

A BETRAYAL OF SMALL CHILDREN OF ALL AGES: INTERNATIONAL FOOTBALL

The first day of the World Cup is the Christmas Day of the sporting calendar, when instead of gorging yourself on all the purple ones in the tin of Quality Street, you could happily feast non-stop on every last nugget of football coverage. The sense of splendour and possibility engages the small child in all of us, eyeing the first match as we once did the bike-shaped parcel in the living room, waiting for the clock to get a move on. At some point a rotund FIFA suit will appear, better dressed than Uncle Horace but still chuntering on about how nice it is to all be here together, even though you know he'll only stay for lunch. You smile and nod. Nothing can ruin this day. The World Cup!

That feeling, you suspect, will persist through our lifetime – but increasingly it exists in the face of all reason. In the past, a poor World Cup came but once a generation. Now they come once every four years. Even Brazil, *Brazil*, the rest of the world's glamorous second team, are rubbish. The greatest show on earth has become the greatest sham on turf, a 'busted flush', according to Simon Barnes, of *The Times*: 'We must face the fact. The World Cup no longer delivers.'

Against those who argue that there is no such thing as a bad World Cup (and they clearly haven't been watching properly since 1998), there are those who say that the international competition is dead *per se*. There are reasonable grounds for that, given how obviously players and managers now prioritise club football – players who would try and run off a gunshot wound in a Premier League tie withdraw from internationals with a headache. Come the tournament proper, it's often a case of fitness – by the time they finish a marathon domestic season (those at England's top five clubs in 2010/11 could have played anything between 53 and 61 games in all competitions), players often arrive absolutely shattered for the World Cup or European Championship, if they arrive at all. The number of top players who have missed major tournaments because of injury has grown exponentially in the last 15 or 20 years, and we've become accustomed to watching players struggling on while palpably unfit.

In truth, there are numerous reasons why the World Cup lacks the lustre of old, many of them covered elsewhere in this book: the negativity of coaches, TV saturation, the disingenuousness of players. As the showcase for world football, the World Cup cannot help but suffer the same ills – magnify them, in most cases. The World Cup was once thrillingly exotic, an unparalleled step into the unknown. New stars would burst into our lives, the first we knew about it from the rows of ludicrous haircuts in our Panini sticker albums, before they would come to life on our screen in glorious Technicolor (see Chapter One). In the autumn term of 1986, one of the authors (we shan't embarrass him by revealing his name) would answer only to the name 'Belanov', the result of a minor obsession with the USSR striker Igor Belanov, who scored a hat-trick against Belgium in Mexico that summer. An equivalent in 2010 might have been Thomas Müller, the revelatory German right-winger, but the kids of today would have known all about him because of his exposure during Bayern Munich's run in the Champions League, or from playing *Championship Manager*. With the right satellite subscription, they could have watched him every week in the Bundesliga, too.

FIFA is unlikely to do anything about the progressively wanton romp with commercial interests, either. The world governing body made £388 million profit between 2006 and 2010 and has lined up more corporate sponsors for Brazil 2014 than there used to be competing nations in the tournament itself. In that four-year period it spent twice as much on its own operating costs as it did on its Financial Assistance Programme for member nations. When it began haggling with the European Club Association over the 2014 renewal of the international calendar, FIFA fighting to preserve the diary as it is, the ECA looking to reduce its commitment to international football, the concern of both was, essentially, their bank balance. The commercialisation of football is never more evident than during the World Cup, which, like everything else, is now about money, not football. It's a betrayal of small children – of all ages – around the world.

If sporting excellence was the name of the game, the World Cup would never have been allowed to develop such considerable girth. Much like the Champions League, the tournament has repeatedly let out its belt, beginning in 1930 with 13 countries (18 matches), rising to 16 countries in 1934, and again in 1982 to 24 (52 matches). A World Cup should be taut and lean, like its competitors; at the current 32 teams, it is a flabby mess of 64 matches, which is far too many. A great tournament should leave us wanting more, like brilliantly honed sitcoms – think *The Office* or *Fawlty Towers* – not go on and on like *My Family*, until the ending is a blessed relief for all concerned. Some growth was inevitable: there are many more nations competing in international football today than there were in the early years. In 1954, FIFA had 84 members; now it has 208. Yet too many teams means too much mediocrity and, while a World Cup will always have at least one dud – that is part of its charm – it should not be heavily populated with them.

The expanded World Cup format also (probably not unintentionally) helps to mask any failings of major footballing nations, for whom qualification is pretty much a given. Since the World Cup changed to 32 teams in 1998, Holland (2002) is the only major country to have failed to qualify. Contrast that with the era of 16 and 24 teams, when Argentina, France, England, Spain and Holland all failed to make it at various stages. This is as it should be. Watching a superpower fight for its life is one of sport's most compelling sights, yet we so rarely see that in qualification these days. That's what made Argentina's shambolic 2010 campaign under the management of Diego Maradona so morbidly fascinating. Yet despite losing six out of 16 games, Argentina still qualified with a little bit to spare. These days, the margin for error is gigantic.

Even in 2001, when David Beckham scored that life-changing free kick against Greece to put England into the

World Cup, there would still have been the cushion of a play-off had he not done so. Contrast that with England's qualification for Italia 90, still the standout tournament for modern English football. They reached the tournament without conceding a single goal in all six games against Sweden, Poland and Albania, yet had Ryszard Tarasiewicz's vicious long-range shot gone in rather than striking the bar in injury time of the final match, away to Poland, England would not have made it on to the plane. You had to work desperately hard to qualify – and quite right, too; it is supposed to be 'the finals' of an elite tournament for the very best. It makes sense to set a guest list of 24, which strikes a balance between the open-door policy of the current tournament and the slightly excessive exclusivity of a 16-team World Cup, the choice of most traditionalists.

(While we're on the subject of size, 24 is certainly not a good number for the European Championship, but from 2016 it will be contested by 24 teams, making it three-quarters of the size of the World Cup from a federation with less than a quarter of its members. That's a whopping six-fold increase on when it first started. Twenty-four teams? You'll have to work exceptionally hard not to qualify – a ridiculous 45% of the member nations will compete at *the finals*; it's akin to giving someone a prize at school for spelling their own name correctly. Still, at least there are enough UEFA nations to fill a 24-team tournament. CONMEBOL had to invite sides from outside of South America in order to fill out the Copa America roster to 12. At first they picked sides from North and Central America, a dubious but kind of understandable approach: Mexico and the United States; then came Canada, Honduras and Costa Rica. Then they expanded their horizons to Japan. When Japan had to pull out of the 2011 tournament following a devastating earthquake and tsunami, their place was offered to Spain, who turned this preposterous act of cultural vandalism down. Spain could have been World, European and South American champions at the same time. Try explaining that one to a Martian.)

There are so many different ways to measure a football tournament, but surely the most important, the most fundamental, is the quality of the football. A plus-sized tournament might not be so bad if the games were half-decent, but in the modern era, there is simply a dearth of epic matches. Gone are the days of Italy's 4–3 semi-final triumph over West Germany in 1970 (they were then beaten 4–1 by a Pelé-inspired Brazil in the final), Hungary's 4–2 defeat of Uruguay, also at the penultimate stage in 1954 (they too went on to lose a classic final – 3–2 to West Germany), even England's much more recent second-round meeting with Argentina, in 1998 (the match finished 2–2 before the inevitable defeat on penalties). From the last three World Cups, only the semi-final between Italy and Germany in 2006 has a case for inclusion in the pantheon. Italy won 2–0 in extra time after an enthralling but goalless 90 minutes (neatly demonstrating that goals are important, but not essential). That is the only 21st-century game that Cris Freddi, Britain's premier football historian, includes in his list of the ten greatest World Cup matches. Equally, when *World Soccer* magazine asked a series of experts to vote for the 20 greatest football matches of all time in 2007, ten World Cup games made the cut. Yet only Italy v Germany occurred after 1990.

The 1990 tournament was a watershed in World Cup history, the point at which the qualities of the old gave way to the quandaries of the new. It is celebrated for flash-points such as a quite brilliant second-round match between eventual champions West Germany and Holland, Cameroon's unlikely and heroic passage to the quarter-finals (including a shock win against defending champions Argentina) before losing 3–2 in extra time to England, and England fans can hardly forget their own penalty defeat to West Germany in the following round on that night in Turin. Yet 1990 is remembered, too, for the start of a sharp decline in the standard of the World Cup's showpiece night. Argentina bored and disgusted the football world in equal measure in that final – a game full of niggling fouls and cynical sportsmanship which is infamous for producing a first-ever World Cup final red card (for Argentina's Pedro Monzón, following, it has to be said, one of the most egregious dives ever by Germany's Jürgen Klinsmann, who, at one stage in the charade, looks as though he is body-popping).

The 1990 final finished 1–0 to the Germans. Prior to 1990, World Cup finals had averaged a rip-roaring 4.69 goals per game, and there had never been a red card in 13 matches; since then there have been a mere 1.5 goals per final (the 1990 tournament as a whole produced a record low goals-per-game average of 2.21), and five red cards in six matches. The modern commitment to victory before glory is never more acute than in a World Cup final, when teams will do absolutely anything to win (or at least, not to lose; two, almost three, of the last six finals went to penalties). The miserable combination of defensive tactics and cynical (if not plain dirty) play has conspired, since 1990, to produce two decades of utterly unremarkable World Cup finals, with only Brazil v Germany in 2002 an above-average match. If that was an excellent and underrated game, the others have been poor. Holland (and, in their own snide way, Spain) were disgraceful in 2010; the 1994 game seemed to go on longer than *Das Boot*; in 1998, the match was completely overshadowed by Ronaldo's pre-match illness. The mediocre 2006 final between Italy and France is memorable only for Zinedine Zidane's headbutt on Marco Materazzi, and his long walk past the trophy having been sent off.

If there is anywhere that fans are more aware of the changes to the World Cup than most, it is in Britain, where it will be a long while before England fail to qualify, and where, despite the increased ease of qualification, Scotland show no real signs of reaching the tournament for the first time since 1998. Neither is a good thing. England at recent World Cups have been frequently poor on the pitch and surrounded by the infantile hubris of the English media off it. When England go out of the tournament, there must always be someone to blame, whether it's Cristiano Ronaldo – 'Winker!' – or the 'lottery' of penalties. (If penalties were a lottery, rather than a viciously strict test of technique and nerve that England have consistently failed, the laws of probability suggest that England would have more than a 0% success ratio at World Cups and a 17% ratio in major tournaments.) Scotland, by contrast, are a sad loss, because their relationship with the World Cup is one of the greatest and saddest love stories of our time. They hold the record for most World Cup appearances (eight) without getting past the first round, and have usually found umpteen weird and wonderful ways to be eliminated. In 1974 they were the only unbeaten team in the entire tournament; then there was Johnny Rep's long-ranger for the Dutch in 1978; Alan Hansen and Willie Miller running into each other in 1982; Taffarel's stunning last-minute save from Mo Johnston in 1990. For decades Scotland have had their heart broken by the World Cup but, even though they have never gone past first base, they keep coming back for more with puppy-dog enthusiasm. It's the same enthusiasm we see from fans on the first day of the tournament, and it would be nice to see it mirrored on the field. It has disappeared from the faces of many teams, and even the fans are finding it increasingly difficult to justify.

CHAPTER 4

POWERS THAT BE

'If you want to test a man's character,' said Abraham Lincoln, who has probably never kept shoddier company than he does in this chapter, 'give him power.' It's the fail-safe way to find out where on the scale between saintliness and utter bastardliness someone sits, a kind of litmus paper for corruptibility. Saying no to the inevitable kickbacks that come with power requires humility and even a faintly noble sense of purpose. On the whole, it seems those in charge of football are a bit like those in charge of politics: kidding themselves that they're doing this for the game, when really the game is doing it for them. It has probably always been like this, but it's worth more than a Rover 75 and a box of Cuban cigars these days.

YOU DON'T HAVE TO BE CRAZY
TO WORK HERE...

Few fans understand the extremes of club ownership better than those of Doncaster Rovers. On August 15th 1998, they watched their side lose 1–0 away to Dover Athletic on the first day of the Unibond Conference season. They'd been relegated from the Football League with four wins in 46 and a minus-83 goal difference a few months earlier, and now here they were, watching a bunch of stringers who'd been picked up on the way down the motorway (three of the four players originally available for the tie had been arrested on suspicion of drug dealing), in a borrowed Sheffield United kit. As they chanted 'We're just a pub team, having a laugh,' the club's former chairman Ken Richardson was awaiting trial on charges of conspiring to burn down Rovers' then home, Belle Vue.

By the time Richardson – described by detectives as 'the type who would trample a two-year-old child to pick up a 2p bit' – was jailed for four years in March 1999, his successor had appointed a new manager and coaching staff, and Rovers were gradually moving away from the bottom of the table. John Ryan made his fortune from plastic surgery, providing South Yorkshire's sub-editors with the perfect vocabulary for describing the transformation he brought to the club over the next ten years; in 2008, and playing in a brand new stadium, Doncaster were promoted for the third time in five years, getting back into the second tier for the first time in 50 years. Ryan had invested more than £6 million in the club he'd supported since the age of seven, but was never short of someone to buy him a pint in Doncaster.

Ryan didn't entirely avoid the temptation to indulge

himself – as Rovers celebrated reaching the play-offs with a 4–2 win over Hereford United at the end of the 2002/03 season, the chairman came on to a standing ovation as a last-minute substitute – but his generally altruistic reign sets him apart from owners who treat their clubs as little girls do their doll's houses; playthings on which to test their ideas about themselves.

Some of the proper eccentrics are, admittedly, the kind of people that make football the game we love. The late, elephant-riding president of Atlético Madrid, Jesús Gil, was magnificently deranged. In 17 years at Atlético, he got through 44 coaches and found all sorts of different ways of threatening the lives of his players, including feeding them to his crocodile. After defeat to Universidad de Las Palmas in the Second Division, in 2000, he announced that the team ought to swim back to Madrid; when they were beaten by Osasuna in 2003, Gil threatened to shoot them. 'I mean it,' he said. 'Some of them don't deserve to live.' Palermo owner Maurizio Zamparini was thinking along similar lines that year, saying he would kill his players, then 'cut off their balls and eat them in my salad.' The closest we came to such entertaining lunacy in Britain was probably Barnet's crackpot chairman Stan Flashman, who enjoyed a memorable relationship with his manager, Barry Fry, in the late 1980s and early 1990s. Flashman was rumoured to have sacked Fry eight times, usually from behind a cartoon cloud of the richest expletives, only to reinstate him on each occasion. Fry later put the figure at 37 – 'the shitbag… I'd just turn up the next day and neither of us would say anything about it.' Though Flashman threatened to beat up players if they turned up for a match he didn't want them to play in, there was a strange kind of charm to the idea of these two fat men swearing at each other.

More commonly these days, chairmen make a mess of things in more mundane fashion: Forest Green Rovers owner and vegan Dale Vince, who in 2011 banned burgers and sausages from the ground (no burgers and sausages! What next? No trainers?), is about as wacky as they get.

Like the rest of society, chairmen can't be bothered with commitment any more. As divorce rates have risen, so has the speed with which clubs tire of waiting for the manager to perform miracles; the turnover of managers has increased outrageously over the last 20 years or so. Until the 1990s, there were no more than about 30 managerial changes per season in English football. That jumped sharply to 51 in 1990/91, and then to 65 in the unusually troubled season of 1994/95, which included Eric Cantona's kung fu kick, George Graham being sacked for taking a bung, match-fixing allegations against Bruce Grobbelaar (he was cleared), and plenty else besides. That isn't quite the record, however: there were a startling 73 changes in the 2001/02 season. According to data from the League Managers Association, the number of managerial changes has increased thus: 213 in the 1950s, 236 in the 60s, 280 in the 70s, 309 in the 80s, 425 in the 90s, and 510 in the noughties. At the end of the 2010/11 season, only five of the 92 managers in the Premier and Football Leagues had been in their jobs for more than five years: Alex Ferguson, Arsène Wenger, John Coleman, David Moyes and John Still.

In many instances, the sackings keep the heat off the boardroom. At the start of the 2011/12 season, the newly appointed Nottingham Forest manager Steve McClaren held 'crisis talks' with the board after the transfer window closed without any of the new signings he felt were necessary if the club was to reach its target of promotion to the Premier League. He'd been appointed after the sacking of Billy Davies, in charge for two-and-a-half years, who made the same complaint... you can trace the pattern back to Paul Hart's saddening departure in 2005, and probably beyond.[10] Davies has an ego to rival the legendary Arsenal and Sunderland striker Nicklas Bendtner, and had a troubling habit of slagging off his own players after the match – the kind of behaviour that makes it all too easy for the chairman to blame chippy managers and dangle the promise of a fresh start under a new man; the biennial changes keep the questions about investment and corridor politics to a whisper. Alternatively, there are the owners who court new managers like Katie Price courts new husbands: there's always something better around the corner. Since Roman Abramovich took over at Chelsea, he has disposed of six managers who had previously won 59 trophies between them, plus another nine they won with Chelsea. In 2011, Carlo Ancelotti became the first manager ever to be sacked within a year of winning a league and cup double; the previous record was five years, and both Bertie Mee (Arsenal, 1976) and Kenny Dalglish (Liverpool, 1991) resigned.

Abramovich's recruitment 'strategy' mainly comes down to his overarching desire to win the Champions League, but other decisions are almost unfathomable. In September 2010, the West Bromwich Albion manager Roberto Di Matteo was one of the most exciting young coaches in English football and Premier League Manager of the Month;

---

[10] As the book went to press, McClaren and the chairman, Nigel Doughty, both resigned their posts following a 3 1 defeat to Birmingham City. McClaren had already decided to go, apparently, in a steaming funk about the lack of transfer activity.

by the following February, he had gone. Foreseeing his sacking a few weeks earlier, he said: 'They used to give you time. Now it's a three-year plan, but if after six months it doesn't go the right way, it gets overhauled. We don't have a three-year plan, we have a yearly plan.' Though it works both ways – managers such as Mark McGhee and Steve Bruce have been guilty of an apparent eagerness to upgrade club whenever possible – it stands to reason that in this climate of short-termism, a lot of managers will prioritise results over style, which means more prosaic football and a reluctance to take the risks necessary to chase glory (were you paying attention in Chapter Two?). Nobody wants to get the dreaded vote of confidence. In November 2010, Internazionale president Massimo Moratti reacted to defeat at Chievo by publicly backing the manager, Rafa Benítez. 'In situations like this, the most important thing is patience. Everything cannot always go well.' Benítez was clearing his desk a month later.

This constant turnover of managers has another, lamentable effect: further erosion of the identity that each club once had. It's not excessive to say that the manager once represented the father of your football club, a person in whom you could invariably invest your faith and even your love. Now almost every club has an ever-changing supply of foster fathers. If one club represents the cultural change, it is West Ham. Between 1901 and 1989, they had five managers: Syd King, Charlie Paynter, Ted Fenton, Ron Greenwood and John Lyall. Changes were so rare that they almost needed royal ratification – in 1923, a promotion season, the *East Ham Echo* declared: 'Syd King is West Ham and West Ham is Syd King. When we talk of West Ham we take you as part of the picture.' After 30 years in charge, relegation turned a depressed King to heavy boozing, and a few weeks after being eased out, he killed himself. There's no time for such intense bonding of club and manager now; in the 22 years since Lyall left, West Ham have had nine full-time managers, one every two-and-a-half years. When Davids Gold and Sullivan acquired control of the club in January 2010, they proudly announced that: 'In 17 years, [we] have sacked just two managers. We're not sackers. We support managers and [Gianfranco Zola, in charge since 2008] is safe. We will bring in players to improve the team in the summer.'

If your flabber's not exactly aghast at the fact that they didn't keep their word (Zola was sacked two days after the season finished), it should at least wibble a bit to find that the board reportedly summoned the manager to his dismissal by asking him to come in and discuss his plans for West Ham, and then tried to get out of paying him any severance by insisting that he was being sacked for a breach of contract. His crime, apparently, was to betray his surprise when told by reporters in April 2010 that the club had put every member of the squad except Scott Parker up for sale. This was all within six months of the previous manager, Alan Curbishley, winning his constructive dismissal case against the previous regime. Brian Clough railed endlessly against club boards, which he considered to be packed with ignorant but wealthy men. A few days after he'd resigned as Derby County manager for the second time, in 1973, he made a typically forthright appearance on *Parkinson*. 'Football hooligans? Well there are 92 club chairmen for a start,' he quipped. As so often with Clough, what seemed at the time a throwaway gripe has started to look like a foreboding.

FORGET IT, JAKE

Despite introducing a 'fit and proper persons test' in 2004 and tinkering with it since, the Premier League has welcomed a number of dubious deals in recent years. Portsmouth had four in one season: in August 2009 Alexandre Gaydamak sold to Sulaiman Al-Fahim, who it seems didn't have the cash to keep the club running and quickly sold to Ali Al-Faraj. Al-Faraj had borrowed the money to do the deal and defaulted within a few months; lender Balram Chainrai took possession, and a few weeks later made Portsmouth the first Premier League club to go into administration. Frankly, the fit and proper persons test sounds about as difficult to pass as your cycling proficiency, and that's before you get into the turbulence caused by heavily leveraged American takeovers. In 2007, Thaksin Shinawatra's £82 million takeover of Manchester City went through despite allegations of tax evasion and corruption in his own country (which he claims were politically motivated), while Human Rights Watch accused him of presiding over human rights abuses in Thailand. The club's chief executive at the time, Garry Cook, set out the stringent criteria Shinawatra had had to satisfy to get the thumbs up from him: 'Is Dr Thaksin a nice guy? Yes. Is he a great guy to play golf with? Yes. Does he have plenty of money to run a football club? Yes. I really care about those three things. Whether he's guilty of something over in Thailand, I can't worry.'

Cook later said he regretted not doing a bit more digging, while Premier League chief executive Richard Scudamore tried to put a positive slant on things when Shinawatra decided to sell to the Abu Dhabi United Group in September 2008 (about a month after he'd applied for asylum in the UK, facing mounting corruption charges back home): 'You could argue that one of the reasons that Mr Shinawatra has decided that it might be right to sell is that it might be at some point he may fail our fit and proper persons test,' he mused. 'Don't underestimate the role that the football authorities have maybe played in that.' It wasn't enough to convince the FIFA president, however. 'These days you can buy a club as you buy a football jersey. We must ask ourselves what motivates these owners and are they really interested in the game, or just making money?' Scudamore must surely have recognised that he was in a draughty moral hinterland the instant the voice of reason sprang forth from Joseph S. Blatter.

'Forget it Jake, it's Chinatown.' The famous last line from Roman Polanski's defining film seems pertinent in a discussion about FIFA, whose behind-closed-doors ways of going about business, even when transparency is on the agenda, do little to encourage faith from ordinary fans accustomed to seeing accusations rebound off a wall of silence.

FIFA has long got by on chiffon credibility, but in 2010 and 2011 the rumours surrounding its dealings seemed to reach a critical mass, barrelled along by the World Cup bidding process. Two of FIFA's executive committee didn't even make it as far as the vote, having been banned by the organisation for allegedly soliciting money in exchange for votes in taped conversations with undercover journalists from *The Sunday Times*, while three surviving members were accused of having taken bribes in the 90s by the BBC's *Panorama* programme. There was talk that deals had been struck between bidding nations, promising one another their backing in return for the same, which FIFA looked into without finding any 'hard evidence'. By the time the 2018 and 2022 World Cups went to

Russia and Qatar respectively – the two potential hosts considered most risky by FIFA's own inspection team – even the Swiss government decided it had best look into sporting skullduggery on its soil. FIFA, however, continued to play everything down, as if journalists had asked about the will at a wake.

The World Cup bidding was followed almost immediately by the 2011 presidential election, with Blatter challenged by Mohammed bin Hammam: the head of the Asian confederation campaigned on a reform ticket; the incumbent promised to split a development fund worth $1 billion with member associations. On May 25th, a week before the election, FIFA decided it would launch a corruption investigation after all – focused on bin Hammam and vice-president Jack Warner, who were accused of being involved in offering bribes for votes. Warner had already had his wrist slapped in 2006, when he'd flogged World Cup tickets on the black market at substantial profit, and was implicated in Lord Triesman's damaging description of the 2010 bidding process. Warner denied asking for £2.5 million for an education centre in Trinidad and £500,000 for Haitian TV rights to be paid to him personally.

It seemed as though secrets might begin to tumble out of HQ like beads of sweat down a furrowed brow, but Blatter was adamant. 'There is no evidence!' he insisted, thumping the table in front of him. 'Stop please to say FIFA is corrupt. FIFA is not corrupt!' Bin Hammam was suspended before the election and withdrew from the running (leaving Blatter to win another term unopposed), and in July 2011 was banned from football for life; Warner insisted he was innocent, but resigned anyway. 'Gifts have been around throughout the history of FIFA,' he said. 'I've been hung out to dry.' FIFA dropped its investigation the instant Warner resigned, issuing a nothing-to-see-here statement: 'The FIFA executive committee, the FIFA president and the FIFA management thank Mr Warner for his services to Caribbean, CONCACAF and international football over his many years devoted to football at both regional and international level, and wish him well for the future.'

Sensing that his organisation's reputation might need a bit of a makeover, the president decided that a group of advisors – a 'council of wisdom' – sounded a good idea. It wasn't quite clear what would be left for them to do, between the work of the FIFA Ethics Committee and a good man's conscience, but he duly appointed the trio of Johan Cruyff, Henry Kissinger and Plácido Domingo (yep, the opera singer – or the Spanish singer, as Blatter called him in an interview with CNN). This might have been the kind of thing the Culture, Media and Sport select committee were thinking about when they described FIFA's approach to cleaning up its act as 'bordering on contempt'.

The favoured line of every governing body – FIFA, UEFA, FAs – is that they just care about the game, man. 'I'm working to have football as a social, cultural event around the world,' Blatter has said. 'A school of life, bringing hope, bringing emotions.' It's all a little hard to tally with reality, however. If they really cared about football's considerable social capacities, they could perhaps stop letting clubs brag about half-term community soccer schools and tell them to make it affordable for those kids to come and see a game now and then, yet paying lip service to football's long-standing ideals seems to be enough nowadays. FIFA 'says no to racism', but when the subject came up in relation to Russia's World Cup bid insisted that 'racism will not be taken into account… it is not an operation matter.' Black players pelted with bananas (it was still happening in 2011) might find it slightly harder to operate freely. The fines that FIFA has demanded from football associations whose fans racially abuse players or other fans are usually tiny, and this is reflected at domestic level. In 2009, Real Madrid fans displayed banners with swastikas on and chanted about gas chambers, earning the club a £2,500 fine from the Spanish FA – precisely the amount it fined Lionel Messi in 2011, when he celebrated a goal by lifting his shirt to reveal the message 'Happy birthday mami' written on his vest. Likewise in Italy, Cagliari were fined £22,000 for the racist abuse directed at Internazionale's Samuel Eto'o in 2010 – the same year Inter boss José Mourinho was fined £35,000 for making a handcuffs gesture at match officials.

What governing bodies seem primarily to be concerned about is money. Blatter's predecessor as FIFA president, João Havelange, set the ball rolling (as it were) almost as soon as he took office, deciding to court the world's biggest companies as sponsors and cutting deals that meant FIFA would make significant sums of money from the World Cup. Unchecked and institutionalised, what might have been excused in the name of astute business has arguably become reckless note-chasing – dressed up as some kind of humanitarian project. Ahead of the 2010 World Cup, Blatter tut-tutted 'colonialists' who had disrespected Africa: 'FIFA is giving back,' he claimed. In South Africa's Mpumalanga province, workers built the Mbombela stadium for 88 pence an hour, with 900 of them sacked for asking for better wages along the way; local taxes funded the construction of the stadium, which was plonked on the site of two demolished schools. Local sellers who had the cheek to put 'World Cup'

resign – the Premier League announced that merely a year after bringing the 25-man squad system in, it had figured out that any player from the named 25 should be available for selection without punishment. No refund for Blackpool, mind.

THE GAME'S GONE SOFT

Tuesday March 10th 1998 was one of FIFA's better days. It was the one on which they told referees that they were outlawing the tackle from behind, in time for that summer's World Cup. 'All tackles from behind put in danger the physical integrity of the opponent,' said Sepp. Few would quibble with the desire to outlaw excessive physicality after the forced retirement of Marco van Basten, whose ankles surrendered to years of abuse in Serie A, and the promise of a cleaner World Cup was a welcome one. But over the years this has gradually morphed into a culture of non-contact, whereby the slightest touch is punishable.

In Diego Maradona's superb autobiography – it's hard to imagine any ghostwriter has ever captured the subject's voice so effectively – he talks about *bronca*, defining it as 'a very Argentinian word to denote anger, fury, hatred, resentment, bitter discontent'. It was Maradona's daily bread, the thing that, more than any other, made him the player that he was, and though it's become clichéd to say as much, if you were to take the fire out of people like Wayne Rooney or Steven Gerrard, they would not be the same players. That fire doesn't merely fuel the darker side of the game, either: scalding intensity enables players of such varying dispositions as Lionel Messi, John Terry, Cristiano Ronaldo and Didier Drogba to reach pinnacles of technical majesty. A certain degree of physicality is fundamental to the contact sport – masculinity distilled to its very essence, demanding peaks that necessitate a rare mental and physical rigour. There is a danger that this intensity is being removed from football.

Nobody wants to see thuggery prevail, and football has improved in this respect since the bruising days when the likes of Claudio Gentile made shin bones quiver, but the balance has tipped entirely the other way. Ray Wilkins inadvertently sparked a football in-joke when, as Sky co-commentator, he repeated the phrase 'Stay on your feet' throughout Spurs' 4–0 defeat to Real Madrid in 2010/11, yet his earnest pleas neatly reflected the fact that, in modern football, defenders cannot go to ground – almost every unsuccessful slide tackle brings a yellow card. Is this really a healthy state of affairs? Part of the problem is that many such tackles look worse than they are, because of the increased pace of the game and the overreaction of players. Ron Harris, the Chelsea hard man of the 1970s, loved to relate how he would often make opponents go 'a bit milky'. Now football as a whole has gone a bit milky, losing its nerve and all sense of perspective with regard to the physical nature of the game.

You can see the shift if you look at how many cards are shown these days. In the 2010/11 season, Premier League referees showed an average of 3.3 yellows per game, up from an average of 1.6 in 1992/93. Red cards used to have serious scarcity value – only appearing once every 16 games in the first season of the Premier League, and in the first 126 years of international football, England had only four players sent off. You were in real danger of becoming a black sheep if you got a red card. In 2010/11, we saw them once every six games on average in the English top flight, and there have been eight England sendings-off since 1998; nowadays, an early bath is nothing to feel unclean about. If numbers aren't your thing, look at what's become of the drop ball thanks to football's new prissiness. The drop ball was once a primal highlight of any match. Winning possession was secondary; this was all about the assertion of masculinity. For fans, there was the anticipation as the two hardest players strode forward; the orgiastic pause as the referee held the ball in the palm of his hand; and then it played out in an almost cinematic slow motion as the ball was dropped and the two players hacked violently at fresh air, each other, anything but the ball, usually, with limbs flying everywhere like a cartoon catfight. Nowadays, even when they are contested, it's little more than a token gesture.

You do not see the same trend in other sports: cricket has reduced but not outlawed the bouncer, while rugby still deals in bone-jarring contact. Football is not a beautiful game; it never has been. It is at its best when silk and steel go hand in hand, along with artistry and aggro, to create the richest sporting theatre. Creation is generally more appealing to watch than destruction, but that is not exclusively the case. Tackling can be a thing of beauty – Bobby Moore's famous interception of Jairzinho, at the 1970 World Cup, is as captivating a few seconds' footage as any. Yet a player in Moore's position today – against Brazil, in a World Cup! – wouldn't dare make that challenge. The risk of a card would be too great. Nowadays the defender's main weapons are pace and positional awareness; fascinating though they are on one level, they will never engage the senses in the way that a superb tackle can. Or in the way that a duel between the artist and the tradesman once did. The contest between Johan Cruyff and Berti Vogts in the 1974 World Cup final is a case in point: Cruyff won a penalty before West Germany had even touched the ball, but long before the end his will had been broken by Vogts, a Rottweiler of a man-marker who tossed him around like a rag doll.

The same was true of Claudio Gentile's infamous man-marking job on Maradona at the 1982 World Cup. Admittedly Gentile didn't so much bend the rules as snap them in four and then stomp on them until they pleaded 'not the face!', but it was still compelling viewing. Every tournament victory has its tipping point but in 1982 it was more a tripping point: after three miserable draws in the first stage, the Italians only got going when Gentile did a number on Maradona – he fouled the Argentine a record 23 times, despite being booked early on – allowing Italy to win 2–1. It's the definitive demonstration of the ignoble art of man-to-man marking; dogs don't hold on to a bone so determinedly. Four years before the Hand of God, Gentile introduced Maradona to the Boot of Satan.

Gentile was one of football's great hard men, a dying breed whose imminent extinction will be keenly lamented by the harder core of football fans. Like it or not, many football supporters enjoy the brooding, bruising side of the game, both as an expression of the us-against-the-world mentality inherent in so many fans, and also for its comedic potential. The former is neatly summed up by the Manchester United career of Norman Whiteside. He scored in three cup finals for United, including an exquisite winner at the age of 19 in the 1985 FA Cup final, yet he says that the thing fans most want to talk to him about is his substitute appearance at Anfield in 1988, when his vigilante menace terrorised Liverpool and allowed ten-man United to come back from 3–1 down to draw 3–3.

A few years earlier Liverpool had had their own warped genius, Graeme Souness, an I'll-see-you-outside ethos on legs. Provided there is no serious harm done, most football fans love a bit of the old ultraviolence – certainly if it's through a nostalgic prism. Stick on a YouTube video of dodgy tackles or an infamous match in your office and it will usually be soundtracked by guilty laughter. Punch-ups are still de rigueur in rugby, or ice hockey, and taking a right-hander without complaint is a point of honour; in football, players stand forehead to forehead bitching about each other's mums, or swap a few soft shoves, and get sent off anyway. Call us philistines, but there was rather more dignity in Francis Lee and Norman Hunter leaving the field still throwing punches at one another.

ARE YOU THERE, GOD? IT'S ME, JEFF

One of the other problems caused – or at least exacerbated – by the excessive clamping down on football's former arts is that referees have become increasingly high-profile, a development as welcome as a group of recently evicted *Big Brother* housemates turning up at your favourite pub. In certain jobs, anonymity is distinctly preferable. Spying. Wicketkeeping. Refereeing. Referees should be stagehands, nothing more, yet in recent times they have taken over from the *dramatis personae* far too often. 'Tring' should sound like a telephone ringing to anyone who lives more than 20 miles away from the tiny Hertfordshire town, but it's a word that immediately resonates with football fans because it's where Graham Poll, one of the most high-profile referees of the Premier League era, comes from.

As well as being thrown into the spotlight by endless television coverage, which demands an ever-growing cast from which to tease storylines, referees are arguably victims of governing bodies' increasingly pedantic attempts to dictate the shape of the game. They're not just umpiring proceedings; they're now the fun-police. If a player takes his shirt off to celebrate a goal, the referee must step in, po-faced, and show him a yellow card (by the letter of the law, he should do so even if a player simply puts the front of his shirt over his head). If a player celebrates a goal by running towards the stands to be enveloped by the bouncing front rows, referees are expected to intervene. If a player needs attention from a physio, not only does he have to leave the field of play immediately afterwards, but he has to wait at a specific spot on the touchline waiting for the referee to wave him back on. In order to do their jobs, referees must be more involved than ever during the 90 minutes of play, and then disappear for the rest of the week, saying nothing. Football is harder to officiate these days – the game is faster, the players more Machiavellian, the rules tighter – and few contemporary officials are fit to polish Pierluigi Collina's pate, but governing bodies haven't exactly helped to keep refereeing from being the subject of intense scrutiny. Often their inconsistent *ex post facto* behaviour, dishing out a warning here, a ban there, only ensures that there will be dedicated cameras trained on the man in black.

It's difficult to feel too sorry for them, though, when they seem to enjoy it all so much; the emphasis on official interference seems to translate directly to an inflated sense of self-worth and a rather tempered sense of humour. During a match between Rangers and Hibs in December 1995, the referee Dougie Smith dropped his yellow card. Paul Gascoigne picked it up and trotted over to return it, brandishing it theatrically at Smith as he got closer; the referee grabbed the card off Gascoigne, then called him back and went to book him, all the while wearing a you'll-not-make-a-fool-of-me-sonny look on his face. Gazza didn't have to do a thing to make Smith look a fool, waiting politely while the referee felt around in his back pocket before realising the yellow was already in his hand.

Rugby refs still use numbers to address players, asserting a kind of innate headmasterly authority that modern football referees don't seem able to conjure. Instead, they're like those substitute teachers who try and be hip with the kids – we've witnessed the referee Martin Atkinson calling Ashley Young 'Ash', as if they've recently become best friends for life – but who must ultimately fall back on posturing. Howard Webb, arguably the best of the Premier League bunch, dismisses gathering players by shaping an X with his arms and then dramatically spreading them wide, like he's doing semaphore, when a simple 'Go away' would do; Mike Dean skips in the air, plants his feet and sticks his backside out to point at the spot from which a free kick should be taken. These theatrical manoeuvres, which can be spotted from space, never mind the top tier, betray their sense that the world is watching them as much as anyone else. Just look at these comments from Jeff Winter after his final game at Anfield in 2004. 'I played a little bit of extra time, waiting until the play was at the Kop end, before sounding the final shrill blast,' he wrote in his autobiography, the obliviously titled *Who's the b*****d in the black?*. 'The fans behind the goal burst into spontaneous applause. It was longer and louder than normal, even for a home win. Did they know it was my final visit? Was it applause for me?' Eat your heart out, Judy Blume.

CHAPTER 5

WE'RE NOT SINGING ANY MORE

In the end, Swindon escaped the Second World War without the ceaseless bombing its industrial landmarks suggested it would attract, but it had been prepared for a pounding. The government requisitioned the County Ground in 1940, installing an auxiliary fire station in the Town End. As part of their duties, the firemen showed local Boy Scouts how to deal with incendiary devices. One of them was Maurice Heritage. 'The firemen were showing us how to do it all, and they had hosepipes spread out all along the terracing,' he remembers. 'It was all so important, but my mind was wandering, imagining the players out on the pitch. It was just the atmosphere... I kept thinking: This is the *football ground*.'

Maurice had been to a single game before war broke out; Swindon lost 1–0 to Cardiff. Even hard drugs don't commandeer a man's common sense that quickly.

When the Football League restarted in 1946, they used the abandoned 1939 fixture list, which meant that it was Cardiff, again, who visited the County Ground first. Maurice had already bought a season ticket. 'I could not wait to get back into the ground for that game. It's a wonderful thing. My first away game we lost 5–0 and got on the wrong train home; we were stuck in Bristol until the morning while our mothers were at home wondering what had happened to us. What an adventure!' Despite moving to Cardiff in the 1960s, Maurice is still a season ticket holder at 84 years of age.

Football has for a long time been likened to religion: each club has its own deity (the team), a place of worship (the ground) and a set of believers who turn up for a ritualised event (the game). Though you don't tend to see banners mocking how long anyone's gone without a second coming, and you'll not often come accross people chanting 'You've only got one God', it does feel like a fairly natural analogy. If you'll permit a slightly cack-handed bastardisation of one of the cornerstones of the study of religion, Emile Durkheim's 1912 work on aboriginal clans is useful here. It might be pushing it to argue that splattering the club badge over everything in sight is similar to the way tribes mark objects with images of their totem in order to make them sacred, but the most striking similarity is in the experience: the thrill of being in a mass of people devoted to the same thing sustains their belief not just in what they're worshipping but also their part in its spiritual ambrosia. He called it effervescence. It's that moment when a chorus goes up and the sun comes out and you scan the crowd and you feel the goosebumps and you hope no one notices the tears in your eyes.

Yet, somehow, religion doesn't quite cover it. In the early 2000s, doctors in the north-east of England reported that more men died of heart attacks or strokes on days that their local team lost at home, while other researchers found fans of relegated teams experienced symptoms of post-traumatic stress disorder to levels akin to people caught up in natural disasters. Before that, a psychologist at Nottingham University Hospitals identified spikes in incidences of deliberate self-poisoning that coincided precisely with Forest's FA Cup defeats in 1991 and 1992. Doctors in Florence found that if Fiorentina lost, it prompted an influx of men with screaming stomach ulcers. These are not stoned teenagers looking for lights in the sky, they're proper, white-coated boffins with reputations to protect, and they say football can leave fans traumatised, hospitalised, institutionalised or dead. Religion? Even Pentecostalism would struggle to offer all four.

Football fandom is essentially a congenital condition – even if you have to wait until you reach adulthood before someone blunders into your life raving about Colchester United to trigger it. As Arthur Hopcraft, one of football's finest reporters, once said: 'There is more eccentricity in deliberately disregarding football than in devoting a life to it.' Besides the visceral buffeting of match days, football is just always there. *Fever Pitch* (and Colin Firth's attempt to capture its essence by wearing a scowl and a leather jacket) has since been bundled up in 'Where Football Went Wrong', but Nick Hornby's description of a supporter's loyalty as 'a wart or hump, something you were stuck with' isn't all that bad. Especially if your parents register you as a club member while you're still in the womb (it has happened). In a study at Luton Town, about 70% of Hatters fans surveyed said football was at least as important to their sense of identity as their family – of those, just under half said their team was actually the single most important part of who they were. Hatters may not be famed for their sanity, but it's not hard to imagine these figures more or less holding elsewhere; at least one tattooist in the UK has had to ink Bobby Robson's face into a grown man's thigh.

Some of the more 'committed' acts of fandom remain hypothetical – to the relief (or perhaps not) of the other halves of the one supporter in ten who would end their relationship to see England playing in the World Cup final – but there's no doubt that the dedicated fan is prepared to endure a number of tests and indignities before giving up. Families are estranged more easily than football fans and their clubs; chances are you've dumped someone with less reason. 'You've got to suffer to watch football,' Paul Morley once said. In a feat of logic that goes through irrationality, spins the globe and crashes full pelt into the doorframe of rationality, the more you suffer – the more 4–0 defeats you watch in the pouring rain, while your car is being towed away – the more credit you bank, even, perhaps especially, as the gap between reality and your dreams of glory widens. Like a bloke who's put his entire week's wages into the fruit machine in The Curse and Burden, you can only walk away if you can come to terms with the sound of it paying out for someone else.

In short, football fans are the marketing man's wet dream. And instead of padlocking the filthy so-and-so's PJs, Premier League clubs have eagerly unbuttoned the fly.

STICKING IT TO THE FAN

The club's cavalier attitude towards supporters is no longer good enough… Although clubs take little notice of what supporters say, they are not averse to pucking them in through the turnstiles in order to squeeze every last penny out of the event. The same attitudes can be detected in QPR's extortionate new season ticket prices, now that they have gained promotion.

It could have been written yesterday, but in fact this comes from issue nine of *FOUL!* magazine, which was published in June 1973. Even with the rosiest, blurriest pair of spectacles on, it takes no more than a cursory glance to see that supporters have never really been at the top of the agenda. The toffs who codified it in the second half of the 19th century thought a partisan audience to an afternoon's football rather crass – this was not a spectator sport but a lifestyle choice (running around: good; boozing and betting: bad). The last thing they wanted when they took their rugged Christian wholesomeness to the flea-bitten masses was to have the pale and rickety fellows who couldn't play barking phlegmily from the sidelines.

In belching black industrialised cities straining to contain their new and pretty miserable workforces, however, the chance to spend Saturday afternoons outdoors having a good holler was one not to be missed. Football's flavours – belonging, freedom, potential triumph – were alien and morcish, and no sooner had working-class taste buds been tickled than commercial mouths started watering. The Football Association wasn't even 30 years old before complaints about ignorant and secretive fat-cat owners (not to mention disgruntlement at the FA's governance) were an established part of the football fan's lexicon.

Supporters' clubs raised a frightening amount of money before the end of the 20th century. Operating like a kind of butch WI, they ran lotteries and tea afternoons to chip in for transfer fees and summer wages; as well as paying for ground improvements, they often did the labour, too. In return they got a pat on the head from the club – if they were lucky. If they were unlucky, the board blithely decided that the new facilities commanded higher ticket prices, or simply took away the keys. In the 1960s, Coventry City supporters forked out huge sums – what would work out at about £1 million these days – building the Sky Blue Stand, on what turned out to be the naïve assumption that they would have tenure.

Fans have long been badly represented – the National Federation of Football Supporters' Clubs, founded in the late 1920s, was a hapless, forelock-tugging organisation so intent on getting into the FA's good books that numerous injustices (including the Football League's insistence that supporters' clubs pay for permission simply to reproduce the fixture list) were fought weakly, if at all. 'To help not to hinder' was the motto it muttered as it backed out of the room, bobbing deferentially. Campaigns have become far more critical, better organised and more forceful since the NFFSC was subsumed by the Football Supporters' Federation in 2002, but the game's governing bodies remain largely immune to the effects. Government intervention has been no better. Even as the true impact of the Premier League was becoming glaringly obvious to fans paying three and four times as much for their tickets, David Mellor's Football Task Force produced little more than a record of the authorities' disinterested red-tape rhetoric. 'Clubs should promote inclusionary ticketing policies and greater accessibility,' they waffled, but actual price controls would be 'inappropriate' and bureaucratic.

Admittedly, there has always been a certain level of satisfaction in the martyrdom of the football fan, stuck in perpetuity as the faithful Baldrick to the game's self regarding Blackadder. But then it was easier to bear when you could still be fairly certain there were such things as 'real football people' involved in running things. People who realised – and were prepared to admit – that football was about the supporters. Not just because they paid the bills, but also because – well, what was the point of the whole shebang otherwise? All the time people like Jock Stein were saying: 'Football without fans is nothing', or managers like Bill Nicholson were dissatisfied with trophies won in a way now revered as *grinding out a result*, gripes about the bastards on the board seemed relatively inconsequential. Even Alan Hardaker, the Football League secretary who could smell a banknote at 40 paces, believed that football's only profit was 'the pleasure it gives millions', and could not imagine 'any club director' seeing football as a business 'fired by dreams of financial gain'.

Once you've finished guffawing, we can go on.

Any uncertainty about how club directors see football was cleared up once and for all at the inception of the Premier League, a Sheriff of Nottingham manoeuvre designed to make the rich richer and sod the poor. BSkyB's emergence apparently meant there was competition for broadcasters. Lo and behold, when it came to choosing which of ITV and Sky would get the rights to live games, they chose Sky, despite the fact that at that stage only 13% of homes had a dish. As a result it would cost fans £72 a year, plus installation costs for the majority, to watch games they could have had for nothing – but the ITV deal would have meant the clubs missing out on about £390,000 per season. Even Faust winced. As the ads don't say: you're not worth it.

In the 1950s, the Football League was spooked enough by fears of diminished gates that it tried to stop the BBC producing live radio commentary; in the 70s and 80s, clubs were still so terrified of what television might do to the game that at least once they threatened to withdraw even highlights packages. If none of that was exactly to the fans' benefit (it's since been noted that the radio ban's foremost effect would have been to deny injured war veterans access to live football), the cost of supporting your club was largely kept in check by the same fears. Only when Associated Television offered a deal that would cover the cost of reduced gates, in 1956, was the league tempted (so tempted that Hardaker missed his father's funeral to discuss it). It didn't come off, but 35 years later, television deals promised to make the click of the remote control as musical to the ear of club directors as the clunk of the turnstiles. Since 1992, Sky alone has put more than £6 billion into the Premier League, and agreements with all media for 2010–13 coverage were worth a total of £3 billion. Going by 2009/10 figures for the Premier League, it seems only Arsenal made more on match days than from broadcasting Blackburn Rovers are hardly on the box, yet made seven times as much from TV as they did on the gate. If clubs didn't always treat their supporters well when they were still making the bulk of their money out of them, the impact of increasingly obscene broadcast deals has been to turn casual disregard into barely concealed contempt.

'Supporters' have given way to 'the market' – in fact, supporters are now part of what clubs sell to the market. The idea of such devotion, the sound of the ground as kick-off approaches, the image of a throbbing, jubilant crowd (which, in real-time, is being asked to sit down): it's all packaged up with the game and dispatched around the globe to people who might never get within 100 miles of the stadium Which may be fair enough; if there are people in Ketchum, Idaho who

170

want to spend £45 a year on Chelsea TV, maybe even £60 on the essential John Terry replica shirt, the clubs have nothing material to lose by indulging their affiliation. But there's an astonishing hypocrisy in the way they are marketed to fans closer to home, who are bombarded with the most outrageous rhetoric. 'True Blades are at the Lane,' according to Sheffield United's season ticket pamphlet, and they will 'reward your loyalty' with frozen ticket prices, so long as you commit to buying next season's ticket before Easter (and, conveniently, before the Blades are relegated to the third division, where average season ticket prices are lower). Or how about membership at Manchester City? If you can stump up £10, you can be a Blue member, represented on the club website by a suitably apologetic-looking chap who *isn't even wearing a City shirt*. Still, at least he can 'feel like [he's] truly a part of City', bless his knock-off club scarf. By contrast, 'Superbia' membership (that's the Latin for 'pride', but the English doesn't quite caress the ego so tenderly – very important when you're flogging something on an invitation-only basis) is for 'our ultimate supporters' and 'the biggest Blues'.

City offers arguably the most insidious example knocking around these days, but it is only an example; there are few clubs who are not prepared to trade on fans' sensitivity to concepts such as authenticity and loyalty. Do you come here often, madam? Have you dug deep enough, sir? How do we know you're a *true* fan? Putting aside the linguistics, the very mechanics of the renewal process force supporters to make an increasingly significant financial decision when their relationship with fellow fans and the team is, potentially, building to its climax, in the final weeks of the season. However well you recognise the creep of market-speak, it's still harder to decide not to renew before you've said cheerio to the east stand for the summer than it is while you're sat watching the cricket in June.

The willingness of clubs to turn fans and the things that they cherish and admire – dedication, sacrifice, stories – into a commodity has been embroidered into the fabric of the game at the highest level since 1992. This is a market. Supply and demand, and all that. But the clubs are not truly susceptible to the pitfalls of the free market. For a start, their gargantuan income from Sky is guaranteed years in advance and includes set central funds (in 2009/10, these amounted to almost £25 million for each Premier League club) besides performance- and appearance-related payouts. This allows them to budget, at least to some extent, irrespective of demand at the gate. It is virtually recession-proof revenue, and at the other end, Sky knows that when people feel hard up, they stop going out and watch telly instead. The latest deal, worth a mind-boggling £1.623 billion, was agreed early in 2009, in the midst of global financial meltdown. Second, calling supporters 'consumers' hasn't so far made many of them behave as such; they still don't tend to choose their football club on the basis of ticket prices. Most would argue that they don't 'choose' at all.

Football clubs are not selling fruit and veg off a trestle table, where it doesn't matter who buys the bananas so long as they're all gone before they start putrefying. In a House of Lords debate in 2002, Lord Faulkener urged club owners to 'see themselves primarily as guardians of a public asset'. When these owners say, speciously, that they're obviously not doing anything wrong because there are still lots of people who want to buy into it, they're wilfully ignoring two things. First, the existence of outfits such as FC United of Manchester, or AFC Wimbledon, clubs founded and run by fans disenfranchised by the teams they used to support as the whims of owners took hold. In the case of FCUM, formed in the wake of Malcolm Glazer's massively leveraged takeover of Manchester United in 2005, Alex Ferguson's response was actually to question 'how big a United supporter they are' and muse, as if the fans (and not the Glazers) were doing something wrong, 'it's more about them than us.' Second, they're ignoring the benefits they more commonly enjoy out of fans' loyalty, and thus any responsibility they owe to it.

Yet they are quick to cry foul on those occasions when supporters find a way to make 'the market' work to their advantage. Like when Karen Murphy, landlady of the Red, White and Blue in Portsmouth realised she could save thousands of pounds by showing Premier League games via a Greek decoder rather than Sky. When found out, she was fined £8,000. If one were designing a sum to scare others into line, perhaps even to put someone out of business in an industry that was shedding pubs at a rate of 2,700 a year not so long ago, £8,000 would look about right. But Murphy took the case to court. 'If I wanted to go and buy a car, I could go to any garage I like. If I want to show football, I can only go to the Sky garage, and have to pay ten times the [European] price,' she reasoned. 'If I don't fight, who is going to?'

Early in 2011 Juliane Kokott, advocate general to the European Court of Justice, decided that it was in the spirit of the Common Market for pubs to be able to choose European feeds; by October, the ECJ had ruled that it was also in the letter of the law (a decision that will no doubt be subject to appeals from the Premier League). Niall Quinn didn't even wait for the decision, however, before launching into a furious diatribe against fans who watch foreign feeds in pubs. 'The illegal showing of Saturday 3pm fixtures involving Sunderland has an extremely detrimental effect on our attendances,' he spat, as the league blustered about the importance of selling on a territory-by-territory basis. Broadcasters needed to be able to 'create services which satisfy the cultural preferences of their viewers', apparently, though pub-goers in Sunderland don't seem to mind a bit of foreign. 'I can point to the evidence uncovered by an agency who covertly visited pubs and clubs in our catchment area and witnessed thousands watching the illegal broadcasts,' Quinn reckoned.

As the chairman of a club that made three times as much from television rights as it did from match days in 2009/10, Quinn clearly has as much at stake as BSkyB in protecting its territorial exclusivity. But as the chairman of a club that made three times as much from television rights as it did from match days in 2009/10, Quinn is on shaky ground criticising fans for watching football on TV. In 1983, there were ten live games per season on British television. In 1992, there were 60. In the 2011/12 season, 138 games will be screened live on Sky and ESPN. If you keep leading a horse to water, chances are it'll develop a thirst.

What should, and probably does, really worry Quinn and his ilk is that supporters (some of whom would previously have derided TV fans as lightweights) are choosing to watch without English commentary[11] in pubs in the shadow of the ground.

TAKE ME OUT TO THE BALL GAME

Football folk are rarely more susceptible to a debilitating bout of nostalgia than when discussing the transformation of

---

[11] Frankly, this shouldn't be held against them.

match days over the last 20 years. Ask what happened to 3pm Saturday kick-offs and before you know it you'll be talking about national service, or school milk. By the time you've worked out what inflation would have done to the price of your 1974 FA Cup final ticket, you've shed a tear at the demise of the penny sweet and become a little heated about how much smaller Mars bars have definitely gotten. Maybe one of Roy Keane's most important career moments was the rant in 2000 about corporate come-latelies, which at least gave us the all-encompassing 'prawn sandwich brigade' with which to express our displeasure without having to age ourselves with phrases like 'in my day'.

But let's be honest: going to the match ain't what it was.

In 1910 a correspondent to *Athletic News* chirruped: 'I'd sooner miss the old woman's best Sunday dinner than a match on a Saturday.' The chances are he'd be missing his roast more often than not these days: in the 2010/11 season, the average top-flight club had fewer than half of its games kick off at 3pm on a Saturday. Wigan were least disrupted, with 66% of matches scheduled for the traditional time. For Liverpool, that figure dropped to 13% – five games out of 38, thanks in part to ESPN's weekly rubbernecking as the climax of the ownership saga coincided with a particularly bleak run of results under Roy Hodgson. In today's hyper-connected 24/7 existence (isn't that what the papers are always calling it?), 3pm on a Saturday seems arbitrary, but it still makes a lot of sense. Most people have already got the time off work, there's still just about time to work a half-day if not, and you can be home in time for your tea. If you've a long journey there and back (fans in the north-east face a minimum five-hour round trip for away games, while the drive to Swansea will take more than six hours each way), you've still got Sunday to wind down before another week at work. And you know right at the start of the season when you'll be free and when you won't, none of this messing around rescheduling things halfway through the season. In January 1963, 7,450 fans turned up to see Swindon face QPR, but under a fresh layer of snow the frozen ground was virtually unplayable. 'The manager sent to the local sports shop and kitted our players out in basketball boots,' recalls Maurice. 'Queens Park Rangers had their ordinary boots and they couldn't stand up.' A fixture was a fixture.

Alas, an impossible dream in the Sky era – why have just one game on telly when you could have five? The broadcaster forks out more than £500,000,000 per season for carte blanche. But do they have to make everything so awkward? After 65 years of unstinting support, Maurice Heritage now has to write off some of Swindon's biggest games, because getting home at midnight is a big deal in your 80s. For 2010/11, Blackpool's trip to Stamford Bridge was moved to 4pm on a Sunday afternoon, ensuring that many fans travelling by train wouldn't make it back to the seaside until the early hours of the morning, with a 45-minute wait in Preston. When Ian Holloway's side later hosted Sunderland, for a Monday 8pm kick-off, Mackems in their cars had to hope for not a moment's traffic and a parking space right outside the ground if they couldn't leave work before 5pm. Those going by train had no chance of squeezing the trip in without their boss noticing – they needed to be at the station by 2.30pm. If they couldn't afford a bed for the night and Tuesday morning off work as well, they'd have had to board the train back to Sunderland at 7.37pm, 43 minutes after they arrived and 23 minutes before kick-off. It's almost like they arrange the TV fixtures without even thinking about fans travelling to the game. Oh.

Man City v Man Utd, Everton v Liverpool, Spurs v Arsenal – they've all been played on weekday evenings without too much incident in recent years, but if the police generally prefer local derbies to be weekend kick-offs to give mindless goons less opportunity to drink themselves into a violent rage, fair enough (although if you keep a set of knuckledusters with your season ticket, you are probably prepared to open a few tins first thing in the morning). But there should still be room to avoid weeknight odysseys: in 2010/11, Arsenal went to Old Trafford on a Monday night but made the short trip across London to Upton Park on a Saturday. Liverpool went to Wolves (88 miles away) on a Saturday but Fulham (216 miles south) on a Monday night; both games were shown on Sky. Who is organising this stuff? Are they the people who need 'Caution: hot liquid' written on a cup of tea?

Mars bars have got smaller, you know. By about 10% – and the prices have risen at almost twice the rate of inflation; it's a wonder British children have the pocket money to get so fat. But confectionery has nothing on the cost of football tickets: by the laws of inflation, your 1974 FA Cup final ticket would still cost less than £9 today. In fact the FA charged £45 for the cheap seats and £115 for the most expensive in 2011. They have that massively over-budget stadium to pay for, of course, but you'd be hard pushed to argue that the quality of the entertainment justifies the charge. Only a couple of finals in the last 20 years have been any good, and that wasn't one of them. Handily, the fact that Manchester City and Stoke City supporters had had to wait at least 30 years for a final – and had recently witnessed a tight draw between the two sides, permitting them to fantasise with the adventurousness of a 15-year-old boy – meant that they were desperate to be there.

Any furore was further kept to a perfunctory moan by the fact that UEFA's scandalous prices for the Champions League final, held at Wembley two weeks later, made £115 sound a bargain: tickets on public sale started at £150 and went up to £225 and £300. For season ticket holders able to get tickets through the finalists, Manchester United and Barcelona, there was an additional price tier of £80. Oh, and the £26 processing fee. Per ticket. For that kind of money fans might rightly have expected UEFA president Michel Platini personally to deliver the tickets – printed in gold leaf on unicorn hide – by swinging in through an upstairs window with a box of Milk Tray, but they turned up in the post looking very much like the kind of tickets that you already begrudge paying £2.50 to book. 'It was a mistake,' Platini said, promising a review. 'It was not easy to decide the price of the tickets because we now receive 200,000 requests for them, and on the black market they cost ten times the price that we decide.' Tout-envy? Oh, Michel.

Pricing structures designed to milk every last drop out of dream-chasing fans are endemic in cup competitions. If you'd wanted to watch the 2011 Carling Cup final without needing mountaineering gear to reach your seat, you'd have been looking at £54 per ticket – if you wanted to be able to see the ball, £70. The most expensive seats were £86. It was not possible to see the Conference play-off final between AFC Wimbledon and Luton Town for less than £41.25, and supporters had a 400-mile round trip to make as well.

Before football became an 'integrated leisure experience' (thank you, FA Blueprint for the Future of Football), deciding to go to the game required nothing more than a pat of your pockets. Keys? Wallet? Right, I'm off.

For a start you could just turn up at the ground and buy

your ticket, a forgotten joy for huge numbers of Premier League supporters whose clubs put up more and more hoops for them to jump through, their talk of the strength of demand lingering somewhere between boast and blackmail. For £10, our sorry-looking Blue Manchester City member gets roughly the same benefits as a member of the Sooty fan club: a card and a badge. It's an extra £15 for ticket priority. Spurs fans have to pay £38 for ticket priority for 2011/12, rising to £44 if they don't want to pay by direct debit. Arsenal fan Pat Riddell has abandoned his £20, half-season Arsenal membership because it was 'practically worthless. Despite the fact the club claim there are 3,500 tickets available for every Premier League game, it's practically impossible to get hold of them.' In the Bundesliga, clubs set tighter limits on what percentage of the ground can be given over to season ticket holders specifically to create more opportunities for people to turn up on the day and support the club. Maybe it's not the perfect solution, but like the rest of the German league, it's done in the name of fairness and affordable access; £30 paid, essentially, to get a login for the online ticketing system seems to be done in the name of making money out of even the thought of buying a ticket.

Much like season ticket waiting lists, for which several clubs now charge. This is, supposedly, to sort the determined fans from the vaguely interested and to ensure the whole thing is properly administered, but there are obvious bonuses for the clubs. Taking £15 from each of the 40,000+ supporters they list in it, Arsenal have banked at least £600,000 for an Excel file. As well as the cash, clubs can launch fan-screwing charges by saying, glibly: 'we have thousands of people *paying* to queue for a ticket.' In reality, of course, the queues are long enough and the sums are set just low enough that the half-interested will still reach for their pocket. One Liverpool fan who paid £5 to be on the list joined it in 1999, and is still 3,000 places from the front. Another, who joined in 2001, is at No. 5,290. In the meantime the cost of season tickets at Anfield has gone up by as much as £340.'I don't have the money to go at the moment,' said Riddell, who joined Arsenal's list in 2007, 'but when I'm 40-odd I should be able to fork out £1,000.'

Being 27,790 places back, he'll at least have time to save up – and he'll need it, given that the cheapest adult season ticket at Arsenal currently costs £951. Football ticket prices have risen by anything from 454% to 1,108% since 1990, compared to inflation of 77%. In the past, a match ticket was no more significant an investment than a packet of fags or a pound of butter. In the 1960s, even an FA Cup final ticket cost about the same as a Beatles single; in the 1980s, it was equivalent to a few pints. In 1990 you could see any club for under a tenner, but within five years you were looking at anything up to £40. Forget the butter, that's your weekly shop.

Recent research by the BBC found that only 12 of England's 92 professional football clubs offered a 'day out' (of fairly modest expectations: ticket, programme, pie and cup of tea) for under £20. It goes without saying that clubs in the top two tiers are generally most expensive – £46.95 minimum spend at Liverpool, £40.30 at West Ham – but there are fans in the north and the south of the country paying £27 for third- and fourth-tier football. On promotion to the Premier League in 2011, QPR raised their season ticket prices by around 40%, and shifted the cost of the cheapest tickets for category A matches up above £40. The board was 'keen to stress that prices are in line with other London-based clubs', but perhaps less keen to dwell on the viability of the comparison to four established top-flight sides. Or the fact that you can actually see the others for less. Before the price reductions announced following Tony Fernandes' takeover in August, even senior citizens were due to pay £319 at Loftus Road for the 2011/12 season. They're old enough to remember when the club used to let pensioners in for nothing.

Clubs argue that they offer good value for money in the entertainment market, commonly trotting out lines about the cost of spending a Saturday afternoon at the theatre, or the opera. You can also fly to Paris in 90 minutes, of course, and the comparison makes about as much sense. It's depressing that clubs should want to bracket themselves with an entirely different form of entertainment with an entirely different history and MO, yet perhaps not surprising when you consider that season ticket renewals at Old Trafford have fallen, but match-day income has not. For now, at least, the club is actually making more money having lost week-in, week-out supporters, the day trippers not only paying more for their tickets but visiting the club shop for plastic souvenirs, rather than goosebumps, to remember it by.

If we really are going to make something of the comparison, though, let's make it this: the Royal Opera House in London sells out its top-end tickets (*La Bayadère*: £420) yet makes sure there are tickets at £15 or even less. There are subsidised ballet and opera tickets available for children, students, senior citizens and families, 'enabling people to attend performances who otherwise may not have thought it possible'; there is palpable concern about where the next generation of *Nutcracker* nuts will come from. In Premier League stadiums the average age is 44, up from 42 in 2004 (since when grounds have also gone from being 95% to 92% full); the percentage of supporters aged 16–24 is in single figures. One in five young people is currently unemployed, of course, but it was the same in the 1980s, when ad hoc research (there aren't hard stats from which to make national averages) suggests a quarter of crowds were in that age group. The ROH subsidies depend on generous benefactors of course, but the clubs can't argue that they *cannot* subsidise outside of the kiddie seats. The rows of hospitality boxes are testament to the workability of scaled price structures. It is simply that the clubs have chosen, for the most part, to direct extra cash into the bank accounts of players, not lower-income fans.

SIT DOWN, SHUT UP

In a hospitality box, there is generally a dial somewhere for controlling the crowd noise. 'Blissful silence' – 'faint chattering' – 'something's happening' – 'full-throttle prole', perhaps, though that last one isn't always available these days. When the Premier League signed up to Sky's whole new ball game, they didn't just get Mephistopheles. They got Ronald McDonald and Mickey Mouse, too.

Football has fallen victim to the creep of what the sociologists call 'McDonaldisation' and 'Disneyfication', whereby a standardised, sanitised approach takes hold: McDonald's is food for people who don't mind a burger that looks like it's been through a spin cycle as long as it always looks like that. Similarly, when in Disneyland Paris to save the cost and trauma of a transatlantic flight with three children, it is absolutely A-OK for it to be impossible to tell that you are not in Florida. But few people require the same anaesthetised, homogenous experience at a football match.

Decision-making should be about more than generating more and bigger revenue streams, and shouldn't seek to tame the game's less predictable qualities beyond the point of common sense.

That a significant number of stadiums needed to change is barely worth a moment's debate; fans were corralled like animals and plenty of them duly behaved as such. Even before Heysel, or Bradford, or Hillsborough, there was a creeping feeling that football was finished unless it could change dramatically. Though it was often thrilling to be in a crowd that teetered on the brink of lawlessness, standing in an inch of other people's piss... not so much. Nobody really wanted to get soaked having schlepped all the way to Pompey, or to have to brave the Portaloos at Millmoor, either, but the hospitality lottery made away days more exciting than trips to off-the-rack bowls named after the highest bidder. Now that Manchester City have banked £400 million (four hundred million!) for naming rights, it will get ever harder for clubs, desperate to keep up with the Mansours, to resist hawking famous old names to corporate sponsors, no matter how tasteless. How long before every town has a Bargain Booze Stadium?

On April 17th 1989, as the country was coming to terms with what had happened two days earlier at Hillsborough, an editorial in the *Guardian* considered the circumstances that had combined to kill 96 people and concluded that the tragedy demanded 'a mighty response to refurbish our football grounds'. The paper was evidently worried, however, that clubs might baulk at the price of assuring supporters' safety: 'Scrapping the terraces, installing all seats, would cost money. So what? The clubs, gripped by market forces, have never struck a balance between transfer fees and civilised facilities for the millions whose five pounds a time make them possible. The paying customer has always come second to a good inside forward.' In the end, and with a bit of legislative prompting, it was actually Lord Taylor's recommendation that they create all-seater stadia that the clubs responded to with most zeal. Although it would reduce capacity, the transition would be a conspicuously costly affair; despite the fact that millions of pounds of public money was to be made available to avoid costs being passed on to supporters, clubs took the opportunity to make significant price rises even before the seats were in. In 1993, Manchester United's then chairman, Martin Edwards, acknowledged on BBC2: 'We knew when the Stretford End was demolished we were losing something like 12 or 13 thousand spaces. We sat down with a calculator and a pencil and said: "What do we need to make up that lost income?" And that is exactly how we arrived at £14, £12 and £8 standing for this season.'

The proximity of Hillsborough and the lack of independent governance allowed clubs to make these kinds of decisions almost with impunity, though Arsenal and West Ham fans were having none of the clubs' 'bond' schemes, in which supporters would pay up to £1,500 towards the cost of new stands in exchange for a guarantee that they could buy a (full-price) season ticket in them when they were finished. Presumably the invites were fashioned using letters cut from *Daily Mail* headlines and Pritt Stick. Clubs continue, however, to work a fine line in turning supporters' complaints into emotional dilemmas. As part of the earbashing he dished out to fans watching football in the pub, Niall Quinn said: 'By doing so, you're not supporting your team, you're actually damaging the progress of the club.' *Progress*. The word doesn't so much play on fans' heartstrings as strum them violently with a barbed plectrum. A few years back Everton fans voted in surprising numbers for a move away from Goodison Park having been sold the idea that the club would get *left behind* otherwise. More recently, extracts from Daniel Levy's open letter to Tottenham supporters regarding the unpopular proposal to move to the Olympic Stadium in east London laid bare the audacious construction of the progress guilt trip:

> ...we have to seek a stadium solution which does not undermine the financial stability of the Club or its ability to continue to invest in the First Team.

[Terrible things will happen if we don't get our way.]

> If you look at the stadium capacities of the top 20 clubs in Europe, they all exceed ours. The new Financial Fair Play rules will mean that we shall only be able to outlay income generated through the activities of the club – increased match day revenues play a major role in a Club's finances and we need to ensure that we are in a position to thrive and to continue to compete at the highest level.

[Do you want to be stuck with the Hajduk Splits of this world? Tick tock!]

> Perhaps more importantly, we now have over 35,000 fans on the paid-for waiting list for season tickets...

[We're only thinking of the fans. Walk with us or step aside.]

…You could say that the one choice we do have is the choice between standing still or moving forward. I know what my choice is and, judging from the emails we receive at the Club, you join me in wanting to see our Club progress.

[Yes, Tottenham Hotspur plc really believes you are this suggestible.]

No mention of how flogging their best players to United every other year helps them move forward, strangely.

Rounding up news from the weekend's cup draws, the *Observer* of January 13th 1935 reported that: 'When the play began and Tottenham thrilled their admirers by a masterful display, their legions maintained a continual roar that was never excelled even on Town Moor in Leger week.' Describing his first visit to Old Trafford in the *Guardian* in 1967, Keith Dewhurst wrote: 'The violence of the crowd (their emotions as much as their pushing and stamping) frightened and thrilled me… those crowds were the last expression of Cottonopolis.' The noise of a football crowd used to be an aural assault, a pounding you willingly went back for, week after week. It was the stuff of legend. The stories never quite agree as to whether it was the Manchester City manager Malcolm Allison or a stunned London journalist, but legend has it that after City's surprise FA Cup fifth-round replay defeat to Sunderland in 1973, the ground staff found someone looking for speakers in the Fulwell End. Whoever it was couldn't believe that the Roker Park roar hadn't had a helping hand.

The atmosphere in modern stadia, temples of plastic, is often fittingly sterile compared to the experiences of old, at times a difference as marked as between a trip to the seaside on a clapped-out bus full of your best mates and a crate of Bavarian Angst Suppressant and a tour of the local 20 mph zone in your next door neighbour's family saloon. There is still scope for some magical moments – White Hart Lane has rarely been as noisy as in November 2010, when the crowd rattled nearby shopfronts with shouts of 'taxi for Maicon' – but they come despite the stadium, not because of it. Before kick-off, bland pop that charted two years ago bounces around the stands, giving everything the air of a youth club, or Radio 2. Worse, at kick-off, they play a club song at such volume that you can barely hear yourself singing along, let alone the stand opposite. Why can't fans be allowed to generate their own noise? During Sky's first Monday Night Football outing, fans on the Kippax wet themselves laughing at the girls sent out to dance to the blaring music. 'What the fucking hell was that?' they mocked. Now the crowd barely get a second to celebrate a goal before the music is turned on full blast.

In all of this the crowds themselves have changed. Not just because they're sat in rows, knees pressed into the seat in front and rapidly losing the blood supply to their feet, though that doesn't help. Those tight rows (not accidentally) encourage passivity – particularly in cold weather, when a standing crowd would hop from one foot to the other, belting out a song or two to keep warm, but a seated one simply tugs its extremities in tighter. Never mind Lionel Messi, it is often the character of the crowd that can't hack it on a wet and wild Tuesday night. The commodified match-day experience has atomised them literally and spiritually. It is not a coincidence that at many grounds it is routinely the away fans that make the most noise; their group consciousness is inevitably aroused when they are so obviously marked out from the rest of the mass. Equally, you could argue that the never-ending roar of the home crowd at the Britannia Stadium is down in part to the widespread snobbishness towards Stoke City's often utilitarian style of play since they arrived in the top flight in 2008, which has sustained a defiant sense of 'us' that is evaporating elsewhere. It comes to something when the biggest stores of fans' sense of collective identity are to be found in the bookshop, under 'Hooliganism'.

The traditional humour of a football ground is faltering, too. Where once Tannoy announcements told Mr Edwards in the main stand that his wife had gone into labour, or that his car was blocking a side road – 'Wahey!' – now the man with the microphone gets overexcited about a penalty shoot-out between a man in a furry suit and local schoolchildren but is better groomed than to engage with the crowd on a more personal level. Football is now too professional – too *serious* – for that kind of thing. This is a corporate production; the billions that have flowed into the game have travelled like an oil slick, coating everything in its path. Danny Blanchflower's glory game has sunk beneath earnest instrumentalism. 'We didn't play well, but we got the three points. That's all that matters, you know?' Got to get to that 40-point mark before we can enjoy this, folks!

Not that football supporters are an otherwise perfect bunch – they are, after all, a people popularly represented by the likes of Tim Lovejoy and Rory McGrath. Between 1951 and 1971, the proportion of Lancashire fans following Everton, Liverpool, Manchester City and Manchester United went from 40% to 66%. If the clubs have been selling plastic fandom, supporters have been buying it, bluffers' guides and all.

Now the stands seem beset by perpetual confusion and at times almost completely unburdened by self-awareness. United supporters draping green-and-gold scarves over the latest official-replica shirt? Somebody's missed the point. City fans getting upset at Leicester fans doing the Poznań, a celebration they'd not long nicked from Lech? What the hell was that indeed? At grounds up and down the country crowds call for the manager to be sacked after four games without a win and they howl self-pityingly about the lack of loyalty in football when he leaves of his own accord, with barely a breath drawn in between. They bellow the unthinkable at players they don't like – just a bit of banter – but throw their toys out of the pram when they get a bit back. 'Will that be seen as inflammatory by Adebayor?' asked John Motson in 2009, as the Man City striker celebrated a goal by sliding on his knees, arms flung wide, in front of the Arsenal fans who'd been on his back for 80 minutes. 'Surely it will.' Surely it should take more than that to reduce 4,000 football supporters to sandwich-chucking fury, no matter how much they pay to be there. Is it really so long since an Arsenal fan broke out of the away end at Anfield to salute those on the Kop who had stayed for the presentation of the 1989 First Division trophy?

Previously we would have characterised football crowds as stoic – in the original sense of the word: not grim or indifferent but able to make the best of whatever the season threw at them. It still applies in places (witness Blackpool's relentless enthusiasm, even as the team slid down the 2010/11 Premier League table and out), but where the money is stacked highest an antagonistic sense of entitlement has crystallized and fans strop about like Veruca Salt. *Give it to me now!* Finishing in the top four is a 'minimum requirement' – not just in the private conversations of board members but over a pint in the pub. The UEFA Cup has Internazionale, Real Madrid, Ajax etched into it, but is apparently beneath Tottenham fans' ambitions because of a handful of decent performances after scraping into the Champions League on the penultimate day of the 2009/10 season. In the era of the filthy rich owner, gratification of such desires must be instant, even when resistant talk of the obscenity of Premier League finances abounds. It's disgusting, but… put your hand in your pocket, chairman!

The balance between schadenfreude and joy is increasingly out of whack. Time was you'd only hear booing when an opposition player had done something appalling. Now Stoke fans boo Aaron Ramsey for carelessly allowing his leg to snap under Ryan Shawcross's tackle. There's barely a seat in the ground from which you can't hear a fat dad telling his own players that they're useless. Yes, they're overpaid. Yes, the rules – which outlaw goal celebrations such as Rafael van der Vaart's hug with an elderly woman in the front row, or Carlos Tévez's bare-chested leap into the crowd – discourage fan–player synergy, but it's not just that. That doesn't explain why fans don't even have the decency not to ruin other national anthems before they gleefully murder their own. There are fans that now jeer their own team if they're not ahead at half-time. 'We should be murdering this lot,' they whine, pointing to the league table like puppies holding up an injured paw.

Things reached a laughable nadir when Arsenal supporters booed the surrender of the 2011 Emirates Cup – a pre-season trophy the club only invented in 2007 – at the end of a 1–1 draw with the New York Red Bulls. Laughable not because they thought a meaningless pot was worth booing (most were keen to stress it was the manner of its surrender, thanks to an 84th minute own goal, that bothered them) but because their defence of the booing was weaker than the Arsenal backline. 'Booing is democracy,' Tweeted one fan, triumphantly, when challenged. Maybe it's to be expected in a country where the last three elections have been won with the support of less than a quarter of the electorate, but this is patently not democracy. It's no more democratic than standing on Westminster Bridge shaking your fist in the general direction of Parliament.

The lack of meaningful dialogue between clubs and fans is a genuine concern – after relegation from the top flight, Coventry City's commercial manager admitted to a researcher from Staffordshire University:

> ...as a Premier League club the apparent need to communicate with fans appeared to be a lot less… your gates are up, your revenues are up, you allow yourself to think things are fine. Communication going out of the club was more about marketing materials with the aim of selling something, as opposed to getting the views of fans and using that kind of information to develop the business.

Some clubs only really concern themselves with what fans are saying to each other, infiltrating message boards to censor dissent or plug commercial interests. It's not good enough. But fans can do and have done better: when Arsenal supporters fought off that bonds scheme in the early 1990s, they did so by filling Highbury with protest balloons and holding up red cards, making their point while adding to, not detracting from, the atmosphere. It sounds schmaltzy, but it worked – around two-thirds of the bonds were never sold. Maybe the relentless progress of the gravy train (or even the belief that it will eventually be derailed under its own steam) has made fans patient and lethargic. Nothing says 'I know my place' louder than a boo.

CHAPTER 6

STOP THE PRESS!

In today's world there is more of everything; there are even more hours in the day. '24/7' has come to refer not just to the petrol station round the corner that will push a box of barbecue briquettes through a little window at 3am, no questions asked, but a society that is permanently *switched on*. First there was 'nomophobia', which meant we all had a panic attack the second we lost mobile signal in a tunnel. Now we're medically addicted to our smartphones: checking our emails in bed, Tweeting on the toilet, and posting running updates on Facebook about what a good time we're having, LOLZ!!!! Which means there must be constant coverage. Of everything. News organisations are checking how quickly – not how well – they respond to events. Whether the story is actually interesting, or worthy, barely matters. Nothing must be allowed to happen and be reported later – technically, that means we missed it.

This is not a world in which you want broadcasters to bankroll football.

In the mid-1990s, Rupert Murdoch set out his (slightly sinister-sounding) plan for making Sky the behemoth it is now.'Sport absolutely overpowers film and everything else in the entertainment genre... we have the long-term rights in most countries to major sporting events and we will... use sports as a battering ram and a lead offering in all our pay television operations.' Between 2001 and 2010, according to the figures from the Broadcasters' Audience Research Board, the number of UK homes with digital satellite went from just over four million to just over ten million; it is demonstrably in Sky's interests to 'go big' on the content that gets them through more front doors. Yet even though 40,000 hours of sport per year makes the subscription seem quite reasonable (really, when you think about it – I mean we must spend £40 a month on the cat, mustn't we, love? No, right, of course it's not the *same thing...*), it is not necessarily in ours.

In 1991/92, the last season of the old Football League, ITV had the rights to show 18 live matches. Football was generally limited to four days: Tuesdays, Wednesdays, Saturdays and Sundays. Then from the very start of the Premier League, when Sky were allowed to show 60 live games, they introduced Monday Night Football. Thursday football became the norm once UEFA began to marginalise the UEFA Cup and clear the decks for the morbidly obese Champions League, and now you can get your Friday fix, too, by watching a Bundesliga game or a Championship match. In the 2011/12 season, a viewer with a Sky Sports and ESPN subscription package can watch 138 Premier League matches, 28 FA Cup matches, 15 Carling Cup games; more than 60 Scottish Premier League and Cup encounters; 80

Serie A matches, plus cup ties; four La Liga matches every weekend, plus some cup action; up to five Bundesliga matches a week, plus a couple of Eredivisie fixtures, the Irish and Russian Premier Leagues, Japan's J-League, Major League Soccer; all of the home nations' internationals, as well as France's and Germany's; the Copa America; England's Under-21s; 75 matches of the Football League; the Johnstone's Paint Trophy, the Community Shield, the occasional match from the FA Women's Super League; Tuesday and Wednesday night Champions League games, Thursday night Europa League games; and Brazil's world tour. Chelsea, Liverpool and Manchester United fans can also subscribe to club TV channels showing live reserve games.

It's not just live coverage that has increased so much. On the first weekend of the 1991/92 season, there was around 12 hours' football on English television, including highlights and preview programmes such as *Saint and Greavsie*. Twenty years later, the slightly nauseating smorgasbord of live football is supplemented by 30 different highlights or magazine shows – on an average weekend, our Sky and ESPN subscriber can watch *Match of the Day, MOTD2, The Football League Show, Football Focus, Final Score* (all BBC); *Football First, Goals on Sunday, Big League Weekend, Revista La Liga, Soccer AM, Soccer Saturday, Barclays Premier League World, SPL Round Up* (all Sky Sports); *Between the Lines, Talk of the Terrace, Bundesliga Review, Dutch Eredivisie Review, Total Italian Football, Russian Premier League Review, Press Pass* (all ESPN); and *Eurogoals* (on British Eurosport).

Even if you don't agree that watching football on a Thursday feels much the same as eating your Sunday roast on a Thursday (i.e. disorientingly incongruous), this is clearly excessive. You could easily watch around 13 live games a week without impinging on your work life (the lack of a social life is a given): one every night of the week, four on Saturday and four on Sunday. The phrase 'all-consuming' feels inadequate – this is a banquet at which even Henry VIII would have scanned the menu, thoughtfully patted his paunch and said, 'Is it too much, do you think, my good man?' No matter how excellent, even enriching, something is, we need the occasional break from it. Suggs understood, musing at the start of 'My Girl' that 'she's lovely to me, but I like to stay in and watch TV on my own every now and then' (for a jaunty ska band, Madness made a mean bittersweet ballad). Even John and Yoko are rumoured to have spent a few seconds apart every year.

The extent of today's coverage of football has two major consequences. First, some lamentable losses (on top of the possible shift in the match-day fan base we talked about in Chapter Five). In the distant past, there would often be only one or two live games per season – it was one of the reasons why the FA Cup final was so magical. The scarcity value was essential. A live match was an event, like a new episode of *Twin Peaks* or *Doogie Howser, MD*; something to talk about around the water fountain at school, or whatever passed for water coolers at work in those days. Even for those who do not choose extreme, all-week sport-watching, the magic of the televised game has long since been obliterated.

Just as tragically, radio has therefore been usurped as the default medium for football consumption. Radio is a format that has always lent itself brilliantly to football – not least because, in Britain, it has had some of the most accomplished commentators, particularly Bryon Butler, and Peter Jones – whose lyrical melancholy as he spoke from Hillsborough on April 15th 1989 was a kind of poetry that few, if any, can match for subtlety and cadence today. Radio is still a vital tool for many of those who do not have Sky, particularly when you're in the car waiting for those magic words – 'And now back to White Hart Lane, where Mike Ingham is watching a splendid match' – but a generation of football fans has grown up without knowing the beauty of rushing through homework to turn on Radio 2 in time for the evening match, a crackly medium-wave reception often coming from some far-flung part of the world. Football will never be more glamorous or magical than it was when we lay on our bed, closed our eyes, listened to the commentary and let our imagination run wild.

Television's devotion to football means there is now no off-season, even in odd-numbered years, when there is no (men's) World Cup or European Championship. It's not long ago that – certainly in the broadsheets and to some extent in the tabloids – there was very little mention of football from the end of May to the start of August. Now we can watch umpteen pre-season friendlies and read every detail about what are essentially training camps. Which means all year round, football forces other sports to the margins – nobody thinks twice about the fact that the biggest stories are invariably football stories, even if something far more interesting has happened in another sport. On February 5th 2011 Mohammad Amir, quantitatively and, perhaps, qualitatively the greatest teenage bowler there has ever been, was banned from all cricket for five years for spot-fixing, yet all major internet sites and news sources led with previews of a mundane Premier League Saturday. (It turned out to be a spectacular day of fixtures, with Newcastle coming from 4–0 down to draw with Arsenal and Manchester United losing their long unbeaten run at Wolves, but nobody knew that at the time.) A year earlier, when England's cricketers won the World Twenty20 – their first-ever global trophy – it was the third story on Sky Sports News.

Football is the pub boor and the pub bore, shouting down everyone else so it can tell us that Nicky Shorey has signed a new contract. In 2011, the first day of Wimbledon, one of the landmark days of the British summer, was June 20th. Overnight, Rory McIlroy had won his first major, the US Open, in astonishing fashion. Yet the lead story on almost all websites and news channels was the fact that Chelsea had made an approach for the Porto manager André Villas-Boas. Even if Chelsea had actually appointed him, it wouldn't really merit a place ahead of Wimbledon or McIlroy, but here was speculation about who would be Chelsea's seventh different manager in seven years, presented as headline news. It's typical of the obsession with anything Premier League. In March 2011, the fallout from a scandalously violent Old Firm game was buried beneath stories about Arsène Wenger wanting to win the league, and Frank Lampard the Champions League. Penned, presumably, by S. Holmes, Esq.

This elevation of the mundane and the inane is the second, disturbing consequence of the explosion in football coverage. Hardly anyone demurs from the norm. Somewhere in the ceaseless race to fill rolling news channels, limitless internet pages and blogs, news values have been willingly sacrificed or unwittingly forgotten. Olfactory bulbs that used only to quiver at the scent of something genuinely new and exciting now fire overexcited messages to newshounds' brains on sight of the words, 'Out-of-favour Manchester City striker Roque Santa Cruz joins Spanish side Real Betis on a season-long loan'. Read all about it!

NO NEWS IS STILL NEWS

'Football is not a matter of life and death,' said Bill Shankly. 'It's much more important than that.' It's the most famous of Shankly's many quotes, and contained a flippancy that escaped many. Whether he realised it at the time, Shankly showed alarming prescience, because modern football is possessed with such extraordinary self-importance that one's first and last breath on earth are made to seem almost piddling by comparison. Football has always been important, even when it was a sport in the truest sense of the word. Look at the two semi-finals of Italia 90: Gazza's tears, and the sound of a nation weeping when Italy went out of their World Cup. Now, however, football has certainly crossed the fine line into self-importance, a transition neatly symbolised by the yellow breaking-news ticker on Sky Sports News. Being masters of ice-cool understatement ourselves, we will say only that it is *possibly* the most evil thing on the planet. This is not an anti-Sky rant – their cricket coverage is quite magnificent, and some of the football coverage, especially of European football, is better than anything else available in England. They do not misuse their breaking-news ticker on Sky News. But the yellow sports ticker has to go.

As children, when the words, 'We interrupt this broadcast to bring you an urgent newsflash' were solemnly uttered during an episode of *Magnum, P.I.* on Friday March 6th 1987, we wondered what all the fuss was about. How could something possibly be more important than watching Tom Selleck solve crimes armed with little more than pheromones and a moustache? It turned out to be the Zeebrugge Ferry Disaster, which killed 193 people. Even in sport, a newsflash should be pretty much reserved for the biggest, most I-can't-carry-on-my-day-knowing-that's-happened events. Yet instead of JFK moments, we get SWP moments. Here's a cut-out-and-keep list of just some of the gems we've noted down the years:

QPR STRIKER HEIDAR HELGUSON HAS SIGNED A ONE-YEAR CONTRACT... LIVE WEST BROM NEWS CONFERENCE COMING UP... INTERVIEW WITH JACK WILSHERE COMING UP... NICKY SHOREY TRAVELLING TO PORTSMOUTH FOR A MEDICAL AHEAD OF SEASON-LONG LOAN MOVE... DAVID NORRIS BID REJECTED... DARREN O'DEA SIGNS THREE –YEAR CONTRACT EXTENSION AT CELTIC... FULHAM DENY THEY ARE IN TALKS WITH BOLTON OVER A SEASON-LONG LOAN FOR DIOMANSY KAMARA...

Making breaking news out of the non-occurrence of events that most people wouldn't care about even had they happened requires a whole new language. The most routine stories are discussed with grave voices and solemn expressions, as if the subject matter were the shooting of an American president rather than a journeyman striker signing a piece of paper: eyes glazed over, voices either speaking very slowly or very quickly. Sport is relentlessly hyped, with attempts made to make every game sound like it'll be out on DVD in the morning. Before he was forced to quit in 2011 after allegations of sexism surfaced, Richard Keys was renowned for such an approach. Even if the game was 0–0 at half-time, with the ball spending most of its time sailing back and forth like a volleyball over the halfway line, he would tell us it was 'bubbling up nicely'. Nothing in football is ordinary, viewed through this prism.

Sky Sports News is intrinsically repetitive, on a loop whether live or recorded, silently rotting your brain. 'It is just so monotonous,' wrote the former England goalkeeper David James in 2011. 'Like being at the dentist and hearing the same looped music go round and round.' In that sense it's the perfect allegory of what is becoming a definitive football news genre: the transfer saga, a unique torture that saps the will to live, never mind the love of football. There have been so many tedious on-off affairs in recent times, reported in minute detail – as if recorded for the benefit of future generations. And which of the year 2350's Football History MSc students won't need to know the hourly change in the status of Cesc Fabregas's move to Barcelona, or the exact thought process involved in Patrick Vieira's failed move to Real Madrid; every single utterance on the subject of Luka Modric from sources close to Chelsea, or the argument in 7,382 articles on why Wesley Sneijder would be the best/worst Manchester United signing ever.

These courtships make it seem like Harry and Sally jumped into bed at the first sight of each other. How hard can a transfer be? Clearly there is a lot of small print, but essentially it amounts to agreeing a fee and agreeing wages. Transfer rumours used to be incredibly exciting, generally being limited to the tabloids – if you saw it on Teletext, as in 1988, when it was reported that Manchester United were after Ronald Koeman, it was cause for genuine fervour. (Not to mention diligently re-pressing 302 for the next seven hours, to see if the move had gone through.) The case of Koeman, who stayed at PSV Eindhoven for another year before moving to Barcelona, shows that the false transfer rumour isn't as new as you might think, but they can never have been more prevalent. During his last year or two at Porto, Benni

McCarthy was linked with a different Premier League club pretty much every single day. By the time he actually signed for Blackburn in 2006, even Blackburn fans must have had to dig deep to muster some excitement. In a media environment where news sense is essentially an obstacle rather than an asset, the most preposterous whispers are reported as fact, eventually dulling insulted readers' disgruntlement to a scoff and a shrug of the shoulders.

The whole thing reaches a farcical climax on transfer deadline day, a phenomenon that Sky have almost single-handedly created and which seems, increasingly, to be sucking clubs and managers into its dizzy vortex. Even those who do no business sit at the training ground into the night, ordering pizzas and sending minions to stand at windows looking fretful, with phones to their ears. On transfer deadline day, even the most inconsequential story is treated as a moon landing, or a breakthrough in the fight against baldness (look, it's big news to at least one of us), which makes it the perfect day to do a £8 million deal for Wilson Palacios (except when an overweight man joins the whooping masses outside Stoke's Britannia Stadium and pulls unimpressed faces over the shoulder of Sky's giddy reporter; roll-up man, we salute you).

Deadline day is, without exception, the most soul-crushing day of all, when the hype-o-meter explodes into a million tiny pieces. Ostentatiously placing a cluster of phones on to the desk, the studio is made to look like some kind of *Minority Report*-esque hub, only one in which grown men fight to see who can make the most preposterous statement. When the Spanish winger Sergio Garcia was linked with a move to England at the start of September 2008, one of the Sky Sports News presenters chuckled, 'that's Sergio Garcia of

Zaragoza, not the golfer of the same name.' Not even straining to remain deadpan, the chap alongside him said, 'On a day like today, nothing would surprise me.' One year they cut to Big Ben as the clock ticked towards midnight, as if to imbue events with a kind of Y2K significance. At the start of another deadline day, the presenter went to a break with the words, 'Deadline day, are you ready?' It's so far beyond satire that even Chris Morris would be sceptical about it.

It is on deadline day that you get the clearest sense of the year-round disparity between how much there is to say, and the amount of time and space there is in which to say it. You've probably also spotted the gap in the run-up to a World Cup, when who sat next to whom on the England team's flight is front-page news. Football reporting has become (often tenuously) football-related reporting, with what actually happened on the pitch frequently demoted to some supposedly grander narrative. It's at its most lurid and visible when professional journalists must dedicate time to wondering whether Ryan Giggs looked to be going grey, having had his expensively acquired injunction turned on its arse by Twitter, but just as reprehensible is the supremacy of the banal. After Manchester United's new-look young side had beaten Tottenham Hotspur 3–0 with a particularly exciting second-half performance at the start of the 2011/12 season, the lead story from many news outlets was that Manchester City-bound Samir Nasri wouldn't play for Arsenal against Udinese two days later. Naturally.

Journalism, as a craft, is under astonishing pressure in the digital age, when managing editors often care more about getting it first than getting it right, and more about unique visitors per month than unique reportage. Slightly perversely, sports writing is probably better protected than many other specialisms by dint of the fact that there is so much coverage; it will take a long while before the considerable numbers of columnists find there is no room for them. But with dedicated daily supplements, rolling news programmes and limitless web pages to fill, a good proportion of everyday football reporting has been reduced to churnalism. For many journalists, the only time they are not at their desks is when they're at a club press conference. As well as making the news wires one of the most prominent sources used – sometimes with minimal additional input – across major outlets, football news reporting has succumbed to the cult of the quote.

The huge amount of time and column inches given to quotes represents a significant change from the pre-Premier League era, since when the old adage – that you never use a headline or publish a story when the opposite is more interesting – has gone right out the window. The media feast on the words of players and managers as disciples on the Mount, despite the fact that parties on both sides have long since settled into a routine, for which all players are now trained by their clubs, whereby one side says nothing very interesting and the other writes headlines that suggest otherwise. It's an intricate dance, and no one's quite sure who is leading: did the papers stuff it up first, twisting something innocuous into an overblown headline once too often for the relationship between journalists and football to survive intact? Or did the clubs just decide that it would be best if everyone was taught to say, 'We're just taking each game as it comes' while earnestly rubbing the back of their neck? Either way, the same familiar phrases are used week in, week out, clubs and writers trading clichés like neighbours dutifully exchanging the same two bottles of Liebfraumilch every Christmas. The practice is so universal that readers will suggest that a well-sourced story cannot be true if nothing appears inside inverted commas.

Part of the problem is the drive to capitalise on footballers' celebrity; it is getting harder and harder for journalists to get one-on-one access to players unless they're plugging something, which has devalued any interview at the same time as making it sought after. PR types make no bones about vetting questions and sitting in on conversations lest they should meander too far towards new ground. Ahead of an interview with Wayne Rooney, one journalist was even instructed not to call the player 'mate', which is hardly the kind of opening that suggests that a full and frank exchange of views might follow. Whether by the interviewer or the PR's design, the most interesting or difficult question is almost always the last.

Most of the time, managers are approached as if they are there simply to address the nation in the style of a member of the royal family, or a wartime prime minister. The situation is now so bad that, after every interview, Sir Alex Ferguson says 'Well done', presumably because the interviewer has made it to the end without forcing him to deviate from the script. He reacts to unwelcome questions with hot-cheeked ire, whispering to press officers about banning a reporter who asked how important Ryan Giggs (mid-Imogen Thomas scandal) would be in the 2010 Champions League final. After David de Gea's mixed start in the Premier League, an excellent European performance by No. 2 goalkeeper Anders Lindegaard prompted ITV's Kelly Cates to ask if the Dane might be in contention to start the next league match. It was post-match bread-and-butter. 'Not at all,' Ferguson snapped. 'I don't know why you ask these questions. You are just looking for stupid little things.' Oh for Ferguson, or anyone else, to be interviewed by Nasser Hussain, the Sky cricket commentator who makes Jeremy Paxman seem slow to get to the point. Hussain doesn't try to whip up headlines or cause trouble – he simply looks his subjects in the eye and asks them, man to man, what the person at home wants to know. It's not only more interesting, it's more honest, in total contrast to football's charade of gentle questioning, which is inevitably followed by attempts to spin the responses into a story.

Some of the spin is ludicrous but essentially harmless, like the story that said 'Real Madrid star Kaká admits Manchester United's Sir Alex Ferguson has tried several times to sign him,' just before a quote from Kaká that said, 'Once he wanted to sign me.' On other, fairly frequent occasions, however, rather more poetic licence is exercised; managers do not simply 'say' things any more, or 'wonder', or even 'question' or 'acknowledge'. They 'HIT OUT'. They 'SLAM'. They 'ADMIT'. In the summer of 2008, Ferguson made some perfectly logical comments about Chelsea's ageing squad: 'I'm not saying necessarily that they're old because, with the modern-day training methods, you should be playing in your 30s. What I'm saying is I don't see outstanding progress in a team that's in their 30s. I think they will still challenge with the players they've got and the players they've added. But I don't know how far that team has got to go.' Ferguson's comments were critical but measured, yet prompted a slew of reactionary articles from broadsheets and tabloids alike. 'Chelsea pensioners under fire', said one paper, 'Sir Alex Ferguson has lit the blue touchpaper'. 'FERGIE TAUNTS SCOLARI: YOU WILL NEVER BE AS GOOD AS MOURINHO', said another. At the end of the 2010/11 season, Spurs manager Harry Redknapp was asked about Liverpool's in-form striker, Luis Suarez. Redknapp said that his scouts had told him Suarez was very similar to Rafael van der Vaart, and was therefore not an ideal transfer target for Tottenham. Mocking stories the next day implied Redknapp had said that his scouts had told him that Suarez wasn't good enough for Tottenham.

RBSOLUTE TWRDDLE

In his 2009 autobiography, Jeff Stelling admits that *Sports Saturday*, Sky Sports News's weekly magazine show, was pretty rubbish in the beginning. In fact his precise words are: 'We would fill *Sports Saturday* with absolute twaddle.' As is the way of things, they gradually gave up on all other sports, and in 1998 became *Soccer Saturday*. Possibly by accident – hardly by design – this is one of few must-watch programmes in football. The be-headphoned Matt Le Tissier, Paul Merson, Phil Thompson and Charlie Nicholas are an excellent quartet, working perfectly in tandem with Stelling, a genuine broadcasting genius. Merson takes unwarranted stick for his occasional mangling of the English language, but he's a magnificent pundit: funny, self-deprecating, opinionated and with the rare capacity for original thought. The whole show works brilliantly, and has a lovely mix of insight, passion, humour and chemistry that strangely has not been copied, not even on other Sky football programmes.

Stelling is not quite so at ease presenting live football coverage, but it's a short hop to Ireland to find the right formula. RTE's panel – usually Johnny Giles, Liam Brady, Eamon Dunphy and Graeme Souness – are intelligent, passionate, fearless and unpredictable, and frequently descend into wonderful slanging matches. They are invariably more entertaining than the match itself. Dunphy can occasionally go too far, but that is distinctly preferable to the alternative. Decent punditry should put you in that most privileged seat: in the pub with an expert. That is precisely what Dunphy does.

These two panels are anomalous in the quality of their engagement with the topic and their viewers, however; for all the enormous technical improvements in football broadcasting in recent years – Tic Tac adverts permitting – the standards of punditry and commentary have fallen.

We know good football commentary in England. Those of a certain age grew up with three genuinely great TV commentators – Barry Davies, John Motson and Brian Moore, not to mention some extremely good ones. Though there are some excellent commentators around now, including Clive Tyldesley, Jonathan Pearce, Steve Wilson, Rob Hawthorne and Bill Leslie, the only one who might qualify as great is Martin Tyler, who belongs to a different generation. Although Tyler is forced to yell 'IT'S LIVE!' before each live game, he generally does not engage in an excess of hype, which means you instinctively trust his judgment when something major happens. Upon hearing him, we instantly have affirmation of what our eyes are telling us: that we are watching something we will remember for the rest of our days. Much like Davies's commentary of Dennis Bergkamp's goal in the 1998 World Cup, when he started screaming: 'Beautifully pulled down by Bergkamp, OH WHAT A GOAL!' The fact that he had last screamed in the commentary box 27 years earlier, when he suggested that 'Leeds have every right to go mad' after a dubious West Bromwich Albion goal, told us just how special a moment it was.

Every broadcaster lives for these moments, but many of today's commentators take a blanket approach, talking up even the most straightforward incidents seemingly in the hope that we'll dismiss what's in front of our eyes and think we're watching a significant moment in football history. Every single week. It means that there can be few technological innovations so greatly appreciated as Sky's 'crowd only' audio option, but it's a betrayal of the very essence of sport. In his tribute to Test cricket, Gideon Haigh made precisely this point: 'Identifying inadequacy helps us recognise excellence.' In Sky's world, any and every game they show is an edge-of-the-seat gladiatorial contest. Perhaps some-where in the back of our minds, we're supposed to think, 'You know, it really would be worth £10.25 a month to watch this in high definition.'

Too much of most modern commentary is infuriatingly glib. The modern offside law, for instance, is often discussed as if it was some kind of impenetrable, malevolent offering from outer space, rather than a relatively complex but entirely logical development that is one of the best things to happen to modern football. Any discussion of offside inevitably ends with the hilarious punchline: 'If he's not interfering with play, what's he doing on the pitch?' It's delivered with the satisfaction of the perfect conversational put-down, when in fact it just makes the speaker look like a smug idiot. It is perhaps an inevitable consequence of the embrace of conversational co-commentary, which no longer demands that the summariser shuts up for long enough to spot something interesting, but instead asks him to yap constantly with the main commentator as if the pair of them are trying to pass time at the bus stop. Stepping into Andy Gray's shoes (also shown the door in the wake of the same allegations that cost Richard Keys his job in early 2011), Ray Wilkins was actually quite good to begin with, making the same fastidious start most of us would to a new post. After a few weeks of on-the-job training, however, the former Chelsea coach had perfected his ability to add very little: 'Haha, you're right about that, Martin'; 'oh, he's over-committed himself there a bit the young man, no doubt he'll have a word with himself about that at half-time'; and the instant catchphrase, 'stay on your feet'. Co-commentators are not supposed to have catchphrases.

It's become normal to shout The Bad Words at the telly when watching football these days, but punditry didn't always give people armchair *agita*. ITV's very first panel of pundits was put together in 1970, the one time they have had higher World Cup ratings than the BBC; Malcolm Allison, Derek Dougan, Pat Crerand and Bob McNab were so popular that, when they left their hotel one day to go shopping, they were mobbed by fans. *Match of the Day*, its theme tune instantly evocative of some of the happiest times of our youth, was something that dads rushed home from the pub to watch and kids begged to stay up for. Women who loved the game watched it for the football; women who didn't watched it for Des. It wasn't perfect, and clearly there's a degree of nostalgia in venerating it thus, but it was a darn site better than the current incarnation, which is stale, complacent and shallow.

Some of the BBC team are fine. Mark Lawrenson is an excellent, enthusiastic pundit, not to mention a thoroughly decent bloke, and would be recognised as such if people could get beyond his occasional lame gags. Garth Crooks is simply misunderstood: if you see him through different eyes, as a classical English eccentric, then he is ceaselessly entertaining. The regular MOTD threesome of Gary Lineker,

Alan Hansen and Alan Shearer, however, offers alarmingly little insight. Lineker focuses on diabolical puns, one eyebrow arched like an ersatz Bond; Hansen, essentially a superb pundit, has been asleep for 15 years and parrots stock phrases like a Twitter bot, with 'pace, movement and desire', 'diabolical' and 'sloppy defending' particular favourites; Shearer has yet to do anything to suggest that he isn't the dull man who announced that he would celebrate Blackburn's title victory in 1995 by creosoting the fence. Maybe we see too much football nowadays to really need it unpicking by a panel of pundits six hours later, but there has to be more to say than, 'I mean this is a great goal, he'll be pleased with that.' It is probably precipitated by the criticism they have sometimes taken for getting something wrong – Alan Hansen has unjustly received pelters ever since suggesting, in 1995, that 'you can't win anything with kids' – but their unwillingness to commit to an opinion of any real strength is a great shame. It's indicative of the drab nature of much modern BBC punditry that when Danny Baker and Roy Hodgson joined their 2010 World Cup coverage and spoke with enthusiasm, passion and insight, they were looked at like aliens. As were some of the players, who couldn't have befuddled panellists (on the BBC and ITV alike) any further had they lifted a glowing index finger and asked where the nearest phone was.

Ignorance is one thing, pride in it entirely another: before the World Cup match between Algeria and Slovakia in 2010, the BBC panel happily laughed about how little they knew of both teams. Licence-fee-payers chortled with delight. French winger Hatem Ben Arfa failed to make Raymond Domenech's final 23-man squad for the trip to South Africa in 2010, but was considered to be one of the brightest prospects in French football to have emerged for years, and had won eight caps before he joined Newcastle at the end of August that year. 'He's a young lad who's come in, no one really knows a good deal of him,' Shearer chirruped on *Match of the Day*. In the 1950s, the Englishman's surprise at Hungary's play was symptomatic of a nation that had for a long time closed itself off from world football, drawing the curtains with a recluse's relish. Today it seems a more wilful failure to appreciate anything that hasn't already been consumed and regurgitated into something we recognise. Thus, when the Lyon midfielder Juninho scored with one of his absurd long-range free kicks against Barcelona in the 2008/09 Champions League, the ITV presenter Craig Doyle called him 'the next Cristiano Ronaldo'. Juninho is ten years older than Ronaldo, has a strong claim for being the greatest free-kick taker of all time, and patented the beach-ball free-kick technique that was later copied by Ronaldo and Didier Drogba.

Around the same time, one English newspaper had a list of the top five players in the FIFA World Player of the Year awards: Ronaldo, Lionel Messi, Fernando Torres, Kaká and Xavi. The headline read 'The best players of the world (and Xavi)'. It was stunningly ignorant, not least because Xavi had been the official Player of the Tournament at Euro 2008. The careers of truly great or very good players like Juan Sebastián Verón and Andriy Shevchenko are deemed to count for nothing because they failed in England, just as the 16 trophies Fabio Capello won as manager of AC Milan, Roma, Juventus and Real Madrid are somehow cast into doubt by England's (not-exactly-new) inability to string two decent performances together. And it's not just foreigners who suffer that treatment: Roy Hodgson turned water into wine in Sweden and Switzerland, but he was only recognised when he performed a similar job at Fulham. English football produces a dismal myopia in its disciples. When Croatia humbled England at Wembley in 2007, their manager Slaven Bilic laughed openly as the English press proposed that no Croatian player would get into the England team. Towards the end of England's utter humiliation by Germany at the 2010 World Cup, the BBC commentator Guy Mowbray sounded on the brink of tears as he asserted that hardly any of the Germans could get into the England side. There was a germ of a point in there – that Germany's team was more than the sum of its parts – but it was lost in such an absurd suggestion.

FOOTBALL HAS A THINK PROBLEM

In the mid-1990s, as the burgeoning Premier League established football pretty centrally in popular culture, we got TV shows like *Fantasy Football League*, with Skinner and Baddiel, and *Soccer AM*, with Lovejoy and Chamberlain. Predominantly sofa-based, they were a bit like an analogue YouTube channel, with added yoof celebrities and, of course, 'banter'. Their hosts ostentatiously rejected intellectualism and embraced televised mucking about. It felt right at the time, as football shook off the stigma of the 1980s, and looking back at *Fantasy Football* (which has been off-air since 2004), Frank Skinner and David Baddiel weren't actually complete buffoons (Tim Lovejoy, however…). Despite all the cheap shots, they knew that Sky hadn't invented football in 1992, and that there were some foreigners who were quite good at it. They simply wore their knowledge lightly.

Now that football takes itself so seriously, however, there's a new strand of coverage that wears its knowledge like a polished bronze breastplate, filigreed with intricate explanations of the deficiencies of the 1931 Barcelona side. What was once the preserve of a niche audience – microscopic tactical analysis, accompanied by chalkboards with pointy arrows and heat maps and pass completion statistics – has gone mainstream, lusted after by national and international media outlets and as fetishised as the Dead Sea Scrolls. As football broadcasting becomes more and more superficial, dry tactical analysis has elsewhere become a shot of Instant Credibility.

In 2006, Reading manager Steve Coppell worried about his newly promoted side being 'Prozoned to death'[12] – exposed and defeated by obsessive blade-by-blade analysis. Now readers run the same risk; the insistence on explaining 90 minutes of football using a single diagram is not only suspicious but also rather joyless, setting the game in a pre-determined template. On reflection, it's interesting to consider the tactical trauma of England's meeting with Hungary in 1953, but in the reports from the time you won't find essays on the geometry of Nándor Hidegkuti's positioning behind Ferenc Puskàs and Sándor Kocsis, or a spray of arrows demonstrating Alf Ramsey's passing range. The reporters were too busy committing to print the colour of the day: the sights and sounds of the crowd; the awe and wonder of the Hungarians at work; that moment when

---

[12] Prozone offers 'in-depth analysis of physical, tactical and technical data' relating to individual players and teams, according to the brochure. 'The benefits given to scouting a team on general and specific opposition performances are unsurpassed,' says Mark Hughes. The 'interactive distribution maps' sound particularly stimulating.

Puskàs puts Billy Wright on his backside with a casual drag-back –'sheer jugglery, this', wrote Geoff Green in *The Times*. 'Wright rushed past him like a fire engine racing to the wrong fire.' Such reports fed the imagination. In an effort to make tactical analysis less abstract, some writers have developed a kind of quasi-philosophical stance, attempting to contextualise a formation or a game plan far beyond the realms of football. No. There are an infinite number of factors that determine a result, but Dutch land reclamation isn't one of them.

The thing is, often it's simply unnecessary. After the 2011 Champions League final, you couldn't move for earnest tactical studies of what had gone on. Most pinned it on Alex Ferguson's decision to field Javier Hernández alongside Wayne Rooney, leaving Michael Carrick and Ryan Giggs to patrol the central midfield, and somehow contain Lionel Messi, Xavi, and Andrés Iniesta. If only they'd had an extra man in midfield! Except that they had, two years earlier, and they'd still been convincingly walloped. The analysis could have started and ended with one thing: Barcelona had much better players. Fretting about formations in this instance is science for the sake of getting wear out of your lab coat. And that's the trouble with the proliferation of instruments available for the diagrammatic analysis of football matches, actually: folk must use them. Sometimes, they're extremely handy; after Stoke have put 600 balls into the box and Blackburn have hoofed 598 of them away, the mass of red arrows that'll show up on the chalkboard helps instantly to convey the point to those who had the fortune to be at the dentist at the time. Often, though, the narrative of a match, or a player's performance, simply won't be squished into a dataset, and the analysis must instead focus on something, some part of it, that will. It's like asking the rest of the orchestra to stop playing Stravinsky so that you can focus on the pounding of the kettledrums. The partial is lauded as the fundamental.

This is the point that Harry Redknapp was making when he took issue with the nation's growing obsession with tactics. 'You can argue about formations, tactics and systems for ever, but to me football is fundamentally about the players,' he wrote in his column for the *Sun*, as the 2010/11 season was getting underway. 'Whether it is 4-4-2, 4-2-3-1, 4-3-3, the numbers game is not the beautiful game in my opinion. It's 10% about the formation and 90% about the players. If you have the best ones and they do their jobs, then they can pretty much play any way you want them to.' After Rafael van der Vaart revealed that tactics weren't really on the curriculum at Spurs – 'it's not that we do nothing, but it's close to that' – there was much scoffing, as if this confirmed that Redknapp was a Sunday league chancer, winging it in the Premier League. Yet you only have to look at the language used by any number of top-flight managers to see that it's the self-conscious talk of *trequartistas* and inverted full backs that's at odds with reality.

DOWN THERE FOR DANCING

'I do not want to watch women trying to play sport.
They only pretend to play anyway and often are a joke so why
involve this peculiar sub-species in our fun.'
(Posted on an article on dailymail.co.uk in 2010)

The internet has largely been a complete disaster, a municipal playground for the moronic narcissist within all of us. The biggest threat to the modern world is not the rise in carbon emissions but the amount of hot air produced online, where the spite of contemporary society is fully exposed. 'You write your snide bullshit from a dark room, because that's what the angry do nowadays,' says Mark Zuckerberg's ex-girlfriend in the film *The Social Network*. It's a perfect summary of the worst football fans on the web, whose most exasperating comments generally fall into four sub-sections: the inane and mundane (what did we do before match reports could be adorned with such insight as 'Get in there Swindon'?), the abusive, the juvenile and the partisan. They are almost certainly a minority of fans, but they shout so loudly that it is hard to remember that. With comment-enabled copy, the internet has brought to written football coverage the interlocutory disorder and venom of the radio phone-in, only without a host to demand a coherent argument or to hang up the line. Have your say? No thanks. As in so many walks of life, a gobby minority has ruined it for everyone else.

Citizen journalism isn't without merit though, and during sprawling news events such as the UK riots in 2011, or even a World Cup, coverage benefits from the information provided by an incomparable number of sources. The inherent appeal of comment-enabled copy is in extending the opportunity for debate to a wider audience, and the fact that readers can comment on the vast majority of news websites reflects the eagerness with which they have 'joined in', as well as the benefits perceived by news providers (increased advertising revenue probably doesn't hurt, anyway). Many people will also recognise how important it is for journalists to be answerable for their work, but whether interactive journalism actually makes for brilliant debate, or a better relationship between writers and readers, we're not so sure. There are certainly some negatives that merit more discussion than they tend to get.

For a start, the environment below the line often resembles not Oxford Union but a particularly unsophisticated playground scuffle. 'As the saying goes, the problem with free speech is that you get what you pay for,' said Aaron Sorkin, who wrote *The Social Network*, of online discussions, concluding that most arguments in favour sound a bit 'like saying that graffiti is good because somewhere in there is a Banksy.' Usernames are weapons of mal-adduction: the anonymous speaker is often a speaker for whom civility, erudition and receptiveness are apparently unnecessary (ladies and gentlemen of the jury: Twitter). The prevailing ethos of football fandom below the line seems to be a malapropism of Clint Eastwood: not that 'opinions are like arseholes, everybody's got one' but that 'anybody who doesn't share my opinion is an arsehole'. This viewpoint is frequently accompanied by the combination of vitriol and arrogance that only the exceptionally myopic and self-righteous can summon. Their assertions wouldn't withstand two minutes' face-to-face argument, but the online environment allows them to dance around the point like David Haye dodging Wladimir Klitschko's fist.

For the system to work, everyone involved must bear some responsibility for what passes between them, but that is palpably not the case. Though a journalist's work will go through several pairs of hands before it reaches the screen, a reader wishing to comment has only to click send, instantly publishing their thoughts. Though there are few sites without a set of guidelines and some form of moderation, the grounds for removing a post are often focused quite narrowly on specific kinds of abuse – and are, of course, acted upon after the event by a relatively small staff of moderators; they don't have time to worry about comments that are simply rude or disrespectful to others. Search the terms 'wanker' and 'cunt' on guardian.co.uk, and you'll find that journalists use the words an average of 150 times a year, usually in quotations. Users are currently hitting the same figure in under a week, with such winning arguments as 'Deal with it you soppy cunts'. This kind of language isn't just casually offensive, it contributes significantly to the breakdown of genuine debate, daring other readers to try and argue yet making no better argument itself than a punch in the gut. It's the online equivalent of inviting someone outside to settle your differences when you're clearly too drunk to grapple with your own front-door keys. It's easy to dismiss as fairly harmless, but repeated endlessly it discourages readers from leaving or even reading more thoughtful input (perhaps it would be helpful if websites asked readers to place their comments into one of two columns: click here if you want to discuss the points made above; click here if you simply wish to assert your club's superiority and/or mindlessly abuse other commentators/the writer/the newspaper/'people'). If it's not all that surprising to find that there are football fans happy to deal in absolutes and hopeless fundamentalism (cf. Chapter Five), it's pretty remarkable that they continue to be given such a stage. Shouldn't we demand more from published content than meaningless quarrelling?

Especially when the impact above the line is potentially just as ugly. Brian Clough, a man accustomed to defending himself, once said, 'It's just an opinion, makes the world go round'; online these days it's getting dangerous to have one.

The responses to comment articles frequently suggest that some readers would rather read the small print on a tube of toothpaste than 800 well-considered words that even gently disagree with their own opinion. While some will take the time to quibble with the writer's reasoning, in a space with all the decorum of the back seat of the school bus, critique has a habit of giving way to senseless aggression. If you approached the Sainsbury's deli counter and directed some of the things that are posted about football journalists at a member of staff, you'd be walked out by your shirt collar and told never to return, but websites need readers to keep coming back and tend, therefore, to police readers' comments with a light hand. Writers are generally considered fair game for all kinds of abuse, on the shaky assumption that because people would cut their own arm off to do the same job, it's OK for them to club journalists over the head with the soggy end. The world of writer abuse even has its own clichés: 'clear anti-[insert club here] bias', 'Do you get paid for this?', and 'Why don't you write for the tabloids where you belong' are all favourites of the genre. For the writer brave enough to express anything so outlandish as an opinion, death threats are becoming part and parcel, as well.

At its worst, the unfettered comments column amounts to a rejection of expertise. 'We live in a society where everybody has an opinion on everything,' said Arsène Wenger, under fire at the start of the 2011/12 season. 'I'm like somebody who flies a plane for 30 years and I have to accept that somebody can come into the cockpit and thinks he can fly the plane better than I do.' But it's not just about hurt feelings; the quality of what appears above the line is at stake, whether it's some writers watering down their articles to avoid any abuse from readers, or others spicing theirs up because they know their work is valued according to how many comments it attracts, not its inherent worth. (These alternate hornets' nest approaches both attract the sneering disdain of some readers, ironically, but risking a few splinters by sitting on the fence, with a steadying hold on pure fact and careful mitigation, less so.) This obnoxious jousting is no good for anyone: under the swaggering sobriquet 'keyboard warriors', the only thing these people are waging a war on is the most powerful and original writing.

It is already apparent that media outlets don't really trust their readers to respond thoughtfully – when sensitive stories break, they often don't open comments at all. No wonder: when the *Guardian* published an article in the summer of 2011, entitled 'Am I in love with my mother?', 83 of the 208 comments it attracted had to be removed by moderators. In light of such figures the modern obsession with collaborative production acquires a pallid complexion; it looks a hollow endeavour. If news organisations were really brave, they'd close comments and print a simple statement. 'You had your chance, you cocked it up. That's your lot.' We'd settle for the return of the letters page, a compromise that doesn't rob the majority of the chance to have their say, but forces readers to make a reasonable and considered argument, to express themselves politely, and generally to justify the time and space given to their opinion. In fact, that would be a good starting point for everybody – perhaps even for football as a whole. Stop shouting for a minute. Take a moment to look around, to listen. The game's the thing.

CONCLUSION

BALANCING THE BOOKS

Throughout this book, it's been impossible to avoid the subject of money; in every chapter, on every corner of memory lane and from every nook and cranny of modern football, money has flagged our attention with the insistence of the class swot. 'Me! It's me! I know! Me! I can explain!' So it seems appropriate to finish by going over the accounts. In this tale of affluence and entitlement, of individual and institutional ego, of a sport that takes itself increasingly seriously but that seems less and less serious about the game, there have been some dubious gains and lamentable losses. If we were to tally them up in a ledger, the books simply wouldn't balance.

DEBIT: *Stoicism.* No more goals like the one that Charlie Athersmith scored for Aston Villa against Sheffield United in 1901 – in freezing, sleety conditions that left even Fatty

Foulke with frostbite, Athersmith played the second half under an umbrella borrowed from someone in the crowd.

CREDIT: On the agenda of FIFA's 2011 AGM: snoods and tights. Ban: actioned! Rules on colour-matching: actioned! Goal-line technology: we'll get back to you.

DEBIT: *Providence.* In 1985, the Scotland manager Jock Stein made Murdo MacLeod (about to make his debut) send a prawn cocktail back to the hotel kitchen. 'Do you get that at home?' he harrumphed. 'Well you're not getting it here.'

CREDIT: Ashley Cole passing a call from a one-night stand to Chelsea's head of communications, Steve Atkins. 'Steve is going to tell you what happens now.'

DEBIT: *Empathy.* After winning the 1950 World Cup, the Uruguay captain Obdulio Varela went boozing in Rio, unrecognised by the weeping Brazilian fans he placed a comforting arm around.

CREDIT: Steven Gerrard arguing with bar staff because they wouldn't let him choose the music. Don't they know who he is?

DEBIT: *Humility.* Danny Blanchflower could be a contrary so-and-so, but it wasn't just that which made him walk away from Eamonn Andrews when the *This is Your Life* presenter appeared with the big red book. 'Oh no it isn't', he said, spinning on his heel. They stopped making the show live after that.

CREDIT: Rio Ferdinand's World Cup wind-ups. There are no words. Not even 'merked'.

DEBIT: *Joie de vivre*. In the penalty shootout to decide the 1976 European Championships, Czechoslovakia's Antonín Panenka stepped up after Uli Hoeness had missed: his penalty could win the trophy, and the cheeky bugger chipped it down the middle as Sepp Maier dived to his left.

CREDIT: Manchester City striker Mario Balotelli being immediately subbed off for a nonchalant backheel that puttered wide of the goal 32 minutes into a pre-season friendly against LA Galaxy. 'Football should always be serious,' said his manager, Roberto Mancini.

DEBIT: *Innocence*. France striker Just Fontaine's boots fell apart in the first training session at the 1958 World Cup, a time when 'We just had two boots, no sponsor.' So he borrowed a pair from Stéphane Bruey. And scored 13 goals as France finished third.

CREDIT: Newcastle striker Patrick Kluivert combing Bnei Sakhnin's pitch before a UEFA Cup tie in 2004, searching for a £4,000 diamond earring he lost in training.

DEBIT: *Genuine competition*. In 1978/79 the English champions Nottingham Forest put the holders, Liverpool, out of the European Cup in the first round. There was no UEFA Cup parachute; Liverpool's European season was over before the end of September.

CREDIT: Clubs involved in the Champions League group

stage bank a minimum of £6.3 million – which includes a £480,000 'match bonus' for each of the six *guaranteed* games played.

DEBIT: *Accessibility*. In the 1980s a 17-year-old could have afforded to get to the match with the wage from a paper round.

CREDIT: January 2011 brought the Premier League's first £100 'ordinary' seat.

DEBIT: *Honest debate*. Brian Clough appeared on YTV's Calendar show alongside the England manager and his predecessor Don Revie *on the day he was sacked by Leeds*. It's impossible that two managers of comparable stature would now sit side by side and engage so candidly, so fiercely and yet so civilly.

CREDIT: The Manchester United manager Sir Alex Ferguson and his Liverpool counterpart Rafael Benítez sniping at one another in a series of press conferences in 2009 while barely making eye contact when they shook hands at the end of Liverpool's 4-1 win in March. He upset my friend Sam! Fact!

By our calculations, modern football has written too many cultural IOUs. Instead of slipping something nasty into the drinking water to settle the account, we suggest the following – a kind of Moral Credibility Purchase Order, if you will:

Governance with gumption
The biggest changes need to come at FIFA HQ; never has a glass box looked so much like a volcanic lair. They could start with simple things, like limiting the number of terms for

which any president can hold office – in the 50 years between 1961 and 2011, FIFA had only three different heads. Sepp Blatter took charge in 1998, in an election that never quite shook off the whiff of corruption; the retiring João Havelange had long since identified Blatter as the man to take up his mantle. It is in the nature of power that it renders transparency suddenly unappealing. Regularly changing presidents would make it far harder for a toadying culture to take hold, and there's always the chance that someone genuinely altruistic will pitch up at the hustings – ideally, no FIFA president should be (re)elected unopposed. It's not that we don't trust Placido Domingo, but world football's governing body could do with a bit of hardcore independent examination. Teaming up with Interpol to investigate match-fixing in the summer of 2011 looked very much like the classic TV-movie response to the neighbours asking about the funny smell coming from your shed: distracting them with the bloke up the road with the droopy eye.

When Eduardo da Silva was charged with deceiving the referee for a dive staged beside Celtic goalkeeper Artur Boruc in the Champions League in 2009, Arsenal submitted a 19-page nit-picking of UEFA's case, insisting that any contact between the two players meant Eduardo's tumble did not – could not – constitute a dive. The player's two-match ban was subsequently overturned on a technicality: UEFA *couldn't prove that the referee had been deceived*. For Pete's sake. No more hand-wringing: no matter what the referee does or doesn't see, or report, if the video footage shows a player has behaved like an arse, he should be punished – not fined (unless they're going to start handing out fines that amount to more than 35 minutes' wages) but forced to sit out a game, with longer bans for repeat offenders. The first week or two of a zero tolerance approach might look like a magistrates' court after a riot, but once the first half-dozen divers had been through the system, players might find themselves suddenly able to withstand a touch on the back. Football is a contact sport, and could safely remain so if players conducted themselves with an ounce of principle. They obviously can't, so it's time for FIFA started justifying its existence.

Rebalancing power

One of the most telling things about Arsenal's defence of Eduardo was the manager Arsène Wenger's assertion that UEFA's case was a 'witch-hunt'. Managers spout this mealy-mouthed stuff all the time; it's a kind of verbal gamesmanship that makes an ass out of men who should command hushed respect, not trip over themselves to defend players tripping over themselves. It's no wonder that the typical modern footballer should be so infantilised, bewildered by the prospect of accountability but damn sure when he's been wronged. Brian Clough once punched Nigel Jemson in the stomach for trying a few stepovers in a Nottingham Forest reserves match, and while we wouldn't go so far as to advocate such hands-on management, the game could do with a few more like Clough's own manager at Sunderland, Alan Brown. He dished out fines if he didn't like the way a man had parted his hair in the morning, and made first-teamers act as ball boys for youth games; nobody could be under the illusion that the manager would indulge any nonsense. Welcoming Clough to Roker Park, Brown said: 'You may have heard people say that I'm a bastard. Well, they're right.'

A bastard, maybe, but Brown was a man of tungsten principle. Before his appointment in 1957, Sunderland had been in bother over illegal payments made to players; everyone was at it before the maximum wage disappeared. Yet Brown stopped the practice at once. In *The Football Man*, Arthur Hopcraft describes Brown's attitude towards bungs as a 'cold, sorry anger'. When parents of potential new signings (Brown had a policy of targeting promising young players) asked for extras, he would tell them they could leave the contract unsigned if they were unhappy with the terms. 'Then they said, "Well, what about a suit of clothes for the lad?" I replied, "If and when he goes abroad with us he'll get his blazer and flannels like everybody else".' One can only imagine what he would have made of the role of agents in the modern game, part and parcel of the gross misuse of player power. Today's lot exist in the age of entitlement, when it is only right to expect more, and better, no matter what you put in. This isn't exactly new – Greek and Roman philosophers covered great piles of parchment with thoughts on the negative effects of affluence, including the sense of restlessness that comes with seemingly unlimited horizons – but it is amplified by the balance of power in modern football, where agents, who stand to gain financially from every new deal a player signs, are not just facilitators but advisers, too. The FA only demanded that Premier League clubs publish the sums paid to agents in 2009, and they have so far been under no pressure to reveal the specific amounts paid to specific agents in relation to specific deals. This kind of information needs to be available for inspection, surely.

Fair play

There have always been exceptional sides in football, and they have always tended to come a cropper in the end.

There's a chance that in fretting about the fate of some of Europe's and the world's finest competitions, we're getting ourselves worked up over something that will eventually right itself, but it doesn't take a degree in economics to spot that it's a slim chance that depends on a catastrophic sequence of events. Across Europe, the teams that now dominate are separated from the rest by extraordinary sums of money and staggering differences in earning potential, which have been allowed to translate almost directly into trophy potential. Any team that disrupts the status quo does so by outspending, not outplaying, the opposition.

UEFA president Michel Platini is one of the only major players in world football who seems remotely perturbed by this, and the introduction of Financial Fair Play (FFP) rules in June 2011 was welcome. The plan is to have clubs breaking even by 2017, with limits on the losses they can post and on how far wealthy owners can go to ease those losses; essentially, clubs cannot spend more than they're making, and failure to comply will result in exclusion from UEFA competitions. Yet it all feels a bit like a Band-Aid for a bullet wound – even before we can worry about whether UEFA has the clout and the courage to enforce the rules: the summer spending of the 32 clubs involved in the 2011/12 Champions League group stage left many unlikely to be able to stay within the margins, before wages are even considered. 'The impression is that not all clubs have really understood what financial fair play means,' said the general secretary of the European Club Association, Michele Centenaro. Even assuming clubs figure FFP out eventually, what would have been a fantastic scheme 20 or even 30 years previously cannot help but preserve and strengthen a hopelessly unbalanced status quo. The clubs it is designed to rein in already outstrip the rest in terms of income, and Manchester City's £400 million stadium naming rights deal demonstrates that they are best-placed to up commercial revenue (and thus their spending limits).

It is implausible that in the 2010s any mechanism could be put in place to restore the kind of relative financial parity that previously characterised the Football League, but there are things that can be done to restore a hint of competitiveness to European football that are a bit more imaginative than 'Let's find our own billionaire!'. The notion of a salary cap has come up every so often since its successful introduction to NFL in the US, with the snorts of derision in the 1990s gradually giving way to more inquisitive noises.[13] To be more effective than FFP a salary cap would have to be a set figure (at least domestically, with minimal variation across Europe) rather than working on a percentage formula, which makes it a fairly radical move, given the financial disparities already evident in the game. The threats of a breakaway European Super League tell us nothing, however, if not that clubs aren't opposed to radicalism itself.

Assuming that that idea founders on the furthest rocks, how about some changes to UEFA's club cup competitions? We live in an era where change is lusted after for its own sake, from small-scale tinkering with club badges (Opal Fruit syndrome) right up to the possibility of playing matches in three 30-minute periods to mitigate the heat in Qatar in 2022; the engorged Champions League can stand a bit of a retro makeover. The security of the group stage fosters a damaging

---

[13] The FA even threatened the Premier League with a salary cap in 2008 as part of Lord Triesman's plan for reform, but like everything else – did replica kit prices come down after the Office of Fair Trading dished out fines in 2003? Did they 'eck – it was simply ignored.

culture of second chances[14] and disproportionately rewards teams just for qualifying; re-establishing a bit of genuinely cut-throat competition – no groups, no seeding – would stop qualification being more than a minor triumph in its own right, and start to address the perpetual financial inequalities in domestic competitions, because even champions might bank only one or two match payouts before exiting. They could afford to sell tickets for the final at £20, and beer for under a fiver.

Imperilling those big fat Champions League cheques might also prevent the same few clubs being able to hoard the best players. It's all fun and games on *Championship Manager*, but what's their excuse? In the Premier League, several clubs are paying players who play so rarely that they barely qualify, qualitatively, as professional footballers. There could easily be tighter squad restrictions – especially if there were fewer games to play even in a victorious European campaign. The 25-man rule seems fair enough (though the fact that some teams make do with around 20, and the supplementary supply of under-21s, suggests it could go lower) but loan deals distort everything. Much like the buy-to-let market, those who can afford to, buy, leaving those who can't with the scraps, or the chance to pay someone else's mortgage by renting. Loan deals could be far better regulated, though it'd require a fair degree of care. There is undoubtedly tremendous benefit to young players going out on loan, but clubs should perhaps be allowed to do so only

---

[14] Tangentially, why must failure be so hard to come by these days? Football is becoming like parents who can't bear to tell their children that they're crap at something and earnestly differentiate down, instead: we've ended up with a third tier called League One, and a non-league division called the Blue Square Bet Premier.

when he has come through their academy; the hedge betting practice of buying a young player developed elsewhere and instantly loaning them out is little more than financial doping. Maybe players of any age who find the proportion of games they have played for their registered club significantly outweighed by those they have played on-loan (the appropriate balance would need to be predetermined and applied uniformly in order to prevent bigger clubs applying pressure to youngsters in this regard) could be allowed to request (or demand, if necessary) a (fee-paying) transfer elsewhere. Certainly, the number of players a club may loan out at any one time should be restricted – is there need for more than half a dozen? – and the limits on the number of players a club may loan on at any one time need to be reduced; any Football League side with ten players on loan (of which five can play at the same time) is building on incredibly soggy foundations. Implemented gradually it could potentially return the average transfer fee to something less mind-boggling, and sprinkle talent more liberally across the league(s).

Fun, please!

We should at least talk about ideas like these, because that-a-way lies proper football that tests players and coaches before it even glimpses owners' overdrafts. In a society whose appetite for gratification is such that it can no longer wait for the end and instead devours the means, criticisms of football's win-at-all-costs culture sound curmudgeonly and embittered: it's become natural to regard points as the be-all-and-end-all, rather than the by-product of an excellent game of football. When Newcastle United's title challenge went belly up after a helter-skelter 4–3 defeat to Liverpool in 1996, the manager Kevin Keegan received a fax from Sepp Blatter, of all people: 'Please allow me on behalf of FIFA, and all those who believe in the spirit of fair play, to commend you for the positive attitude you bring to our game.' Keegan knew that everyone who looked at him in the aftermath expected to catch a gaze haunted by the defeat, but it wasn't. It wasn't enough for him simply to win. 'I turned to Terry Mc [Terry McDermott, his assistant] on the coach and said, "I know I should be disappointed, but I'm elated".'

There is some debate about football's responsibility to enthrall. 'It may be entertaining,' wrote Jonathan Wilson in a piece for the *Guardian* in 2011, 'but it is not and should never be an entertainment.' Perhaps in its purest form, but modern football is far from that. Everything in recent history has relied on the shifting of football into the entertainment business, from the abolition of the maximum wage (immediately upping his wages to £100 a week, Fulham chairman Tommy Trinder said 'Johnny Haynes is a top entertainer, and will be paid as one from now on') to Sky's investment in the game (football was Rupert Murdoch's entertainment leader). Unless you get your kicks out of hedge fund reports, it's downright insulting, in that case, to find that football now insists on being judged as a 'results business', especially given the excessive pageantry of the media coverage.

People power

Go to a Bundesliga game and for about £10 you'll get your match ticket, free rail travel, and the option of standing while you watch the match supping a pint. Between 2006/07 and 2010/11, four different clubs won the title, and an average of only eight points separated first and third; four different clubs won the German cup in that spell, too. They have a steady stream of home-grown talent emerging (six of Bayern Munich's 2010 Champions League final squad came from the youth team) and excelling, collectively, on the international stage. Whatever the appeal of the other leagues' millionaire superstars (and in fairness there aren't many who'd say they get nothing from watching £250,000-a-week players like Sergio Aguero, who aren't in Lancashire for the weather), this is the kind of thing that really stirs a football fan's loins: a competition that sees through their eyes, and attends to things it doesn't like the look of.

The ideas we've tossed around here are more or less plausible, and there'll no doubt be ones we've missed, but the point is that there are things that can be done to recover the spirit of the game; the Premier League is simply too blinded by the glint off its own hype to act before it is forced by regulation or calamity. Fans can't do much about the first but they can give clubs a taster of the second. There have already been signs of a greater willingness among supporters to vote with their feet, with the attendance at Stamford Bridge for Chelsea's Champions League match against Bayer Leverkusen in September 2011 down by 17% on the equivalent game the previous season – after ticket prices went up by 33%. Chelsea Supporters' Group advocated a mass boycott of the next home Champions League game, too. It's fairly easy to understand why some fans might be reluctant to miss a match, but that kind of co-ordinated action could have a significant impact – it was after a massive drop in attendance for a game against Rosenborg in 2007 (down to under 25,000, from more than 32,000 at the start of the 2006/07 Champions League campaign) that Chelsea froze prices for their European fixtures. Marching from a pub you would have been in anyway to a ground you were already going to might make nice pictures for the local paper, but it won't make much difference to the board. An empty ground, however, would scare the bejesus out of them. The game's been sold down the river because the reassuring jingle of coins has always been louder than the protests of disenfranchised supporters; few things could prompt those in charge to act more quickly than a soundless shake of the piggy bank.

PAYMENT: DUE

BIBLIOGRAPHY

INTRODUCTION

Robert Philip, 2001. 'Giovanni honoured to be a hero again', *Daily Telegraph*, 5 November.

Mel Charles, 2009. *In the shadow of a giant*. John Blake Publishing.

Roy Keane, 2002. *Keane: The Autobiography*. Michael Joseph

Matt Le Tissier, 2009. *Taking Le Tiss*. HarperSport.

Scott Murray, 2010. 'World Cup final: Holland v Spain – as it happened', guardian.co.uk/football, 11 July.

Nat Lofthouse, 1954. *Goals Galore*. Stanley Paul.

Victor Hugo, 1864. *William Shakespeare*.

Matthew Taylor, 2001. 'Beyond the maximum wage: the earnings of football professionals in England, 1900–39', *Soccer and Society* 2(3):101–118.

Len Shackleton, 1955. *The Crown Prince of Soccer*. Nicholas Kaye.

Sean Hamil, Jonathan Michie and Christine Oughton (Eds.), 1999. *A game of two halves? The business of football*. Mainstream Publishing.

LIVING THE DREAM

Deloitte, 'Annual Review of Football Finance 2011', June. deloitte.com/view/en_GB/uk/industries/sportsbusinessgroup/sports/football/annual-review-of-football-finance-2011/

Deloitte, 2011. 'Clubs spend a record £225 million in January transfer window', deloitte.com 1 February.

Stephen Burgen, 2006. 'Charity begins at Nou Camp', *The Times*, 11 September.

David Conn, 2011. 'Why Qatar deal has taken the shine from Barca's halo', *Guardian*, 16 February.

Daniel Taylor, 2011. 'Manchester City bank record £400m sponsorship deal with Etihad Airways', guardian.co.uk/football, 8 July.

ESPN *The Magazine*, May 2011: '200 best paying teams in the world', (no author given; accessed online: sports.espn.go.com/espn/news/story?id=6354899)

ESPN *The Magazine*, May 2011: 'Best paid athletes from 182 countries', (no author given; accessed online: sports.espn.go.com/espn/news/story?id=6391145)

FourFourTwo: 'The Football Rich List 2010/11: The Managers' fourfourtwo.com/lists/thefootballrichlist201011themanagers.aspx

Ben Lyttleton, 2011. 'Nasri transfer cements Jean-Pierre Bernes as France's prime operator', SI.com, 19 August.

Ian Herbert, 2010. 'Hodgson's big clearout leaves Liverpool with £9m agents' bill', *Independent*, 1 December.

Simon Jordan, 2005. 'Why I believe agents should be neutered', *Observer*, 7 August.

Dominic Fifield, 2003. 'New Leeds chairman uncovers fishy past', *Guardian*, 21 May.

'Premier League club accounts: how in debt are they?' guardian.co.uk/news/datablog/2011/may/19/football-club-accounts-debt

ONWARDS

Editorial, 1989. 'Hillsborough football disaster: comment', *The Sunday Times*, April 16.

Charlie Brooker, 2011. 'Why idolise footballers? It's like living in a world where half of us worship shire horses', guardian.co.uk/commentisfree, 30 May.

CHAPTER ONE

Duncan Edwards, 1958. *Tackle soccer this way*. Stanley Paul.

Abraham Maslow, 1943. 'A theory of human motivation', *Psychological Review* 50(4): 370–396.

Guy Patrick, 2010. 'What a right Nani', *Sun*, 29 November.

EXCESS 1-0 SUCCESS

Simon Moon, 2006. 'Beckham the worldwide brand', thisismoney.co.uk, 8 June.

Rob Smyth, 2009. 'Becks studies: Staffordshire University 2000', *Observer*, 17 May.

'Futebol Finance: 100 biggest salaries in football 2011', futebolfinance.com/os-100-maiores-salarios-de-jogadores-de-futebol-2011

Anthony King, 1998. *The End of the Terraces*. Leicester University Press.

Jonathan Hayter, 2000. 'For sale... my World Cup medal', *Sunday Mirror*, 3 December.

'One-on-one: Matt Le Tissier', *FourFourTwo*, October 2010.

Ashley Cole, 2006. *My Defence: winning, losing, scandals and the drama of Germany 2006*. Headline Book Publishing.

Gordon Smart, 2011. 'Here we tow, here we tow', *Sun*, 25 April.

'The ultimate WAG-mobile', *MailOnline*, 5 October 2009.

DON'T YOU WANT ME, BABY?

Martin Cloake and Adam Powley, 2004. *We Are Tottenham: voices from White Hart Lane*. Mainstream Publishing.

Daniel Taylor, 2010. 'United in shock as Rooney eyes move to City: Striker ready to force explosive transfer', *Guardian*, 19 October.

Steve Black. 'True Love', *United We Stand*, Issue 35.

EVERYONE'S AT IT

David Lacey, 1990. 'Sparkling bequest of the nearly man', *Guardian*, 6 July.

Sid Lowe, 2011. 'Navarro's shameful play-acting widely condemned by peers', SI.com, 2 March.

Michael Walker, 2006. 'Holland exit in acrimony as four see red', *Guardian*, 26 June.

'FIFA: Laws of the Game 2011/12' fifa.com/mm/document/affederation/generic/81/42/36/lawsofthegame_2010_11_e.pdf

Cesar Torres, 2009. 'On diving: soccer's integrity is at stake', *The New York Times Soccer Blog*, 17 September.

Scott Murray, 2011. 'The Joy of Six: Manchester United v Chelsea matches', *Guardian Sport Blog*, 6 May.

Georgina Turner, 2011. 'Are players entitled to go down? Just think of what we're missing', SI.com, 22 April.

Steven Gerrard, 2006. *Gerrard: My Autobiography*. Bantam Press.

HARDER, BETTER, FASTER, STRONGER

'William Henry 'Fatty' Foulke 1874–1916: English Footballer and Cricketer' bbc.co.uk/dna/h2g2/A3641708

Kuh, G. and Arnold, J.C., 1993. 'Liquid Bonding: A Cultural Analysis of the Role of Alcohol in Fraternity Pledgeship', *Journal of College Student Development*, 34(5): 327–334.

Gary Imlach, 2006. *My Father and Other Working-Class Football Heroes*. Yellow Jersey.

CHAPTER TWO

'The greatest teams', *World Soccer Magazine*, July 2007.

THE PRICE OF VICTORY

Hugh McIlvanney, 1981. 'Bill Shankly, a hero to players and fans alike', *Observer*, 4 October.

Centre for the Sociology of Sport, 1996. 'British Football on Television', le.ac.uk/sociology/css/resources/factsheets/fs8.html

Nick Harris, 2009. '£1.78bn: record Premier League TV deal defies economic slump', *The Independent*, 7 February.

'Newcastle reveal £17.1m loss after stint in Championship', guardian.co.uk/football, 30 March 2011.

ALL DEFENCE AND NO GOALS MAKES FOOTBALL A DULL GAME

David Lacey, 1983. 'Epic tale that bears repeating', *Guardian*, 23 May.

Hugh McIlvanney, 1983. 'Power to the glory game', *Observer*, 29 May.

Alan Smith, 2007. 'No time for fun when winning Mourinho's way', *Telegraph*, 21 May.

Jonathan Wilson, 2011. 'Uruguay find the case for the defence is strangely lacking', *Guardian Sport Blog*, 9 July.

FAHRENHEIT 4-2-3-1

Ewing Grahame, 2010. 'Craig Levein defends his strikerless 4-6-0 formation', *telegraph.co.uk*, 11 October.

Sid Lowe, 2007. 'English teams are robbing game of skill, says Valdano', *Guardian*, 8 May.

Hugh McIlvanney, 1984. 'Greaves gets by on his own spirit', *Observer*, 7 October.

Tom Horan, 2010. 'Should football be considered an art form?', *telegraph.co.uk*, 9 June.

MEN FROM MARS

'David Beckham and the selling of European Football', 13 August 2003. knowledge.wharton.upenn.edu/article.cfm?articleid=829

James Ducker, 2011. 'Training-kit sponsor swells Old Trafford coffers by £40m', *The Times*, 23 August.

THE IRRATIONAL NOSTALGIA CARD

Alex Bellos, 2001. 'How Nike bought Brazil', *Guardian*, 9 July.

guardian.co.uk/football/blog/poll/2011/jun/06/european-goal-of-the-season-poll

CHAPTER THREE

Norman Fox, 1998. 'England's delusions of grandeur: the game which gave birth to the European Cup kicked off 44 years ago today', *Independent*, 13 December.

'History of the Football League'. football-league.co.uk/page/History/HistoryDetail/0,,10794~1357277,00.html

GREED IS GOOD: THE PREMIER LEAGUE

'Barclays Premier League Stats: Team Attendance – 2010/11'. soccernet.espn.go.com/stats/attendance/_/league/eng.1/year/2010/barclays-premier-league?cc=5739

'A history of the Premier League'. premierleague.com/page/History

Brian Glanville, 1991. 'FA's blueprint is a charter for the greedy clubs', *The Sunday Times*, 23 June.

Martin Thorpe, 1991. 'England manager remains unconvinced by changes', *Guardian*, 1 August.

'Football League names Npower as new sponsor', 16 March 2010. news.bbc.co.uk/1/hi/business/8570749.stm

'Barclays renews Premier League sponsorship', 26 October 2009. premierleague.com/page/Headlines/0,,12306~1835324,00.html

Alan Hansen, 2011. 'Constant threat of upsets lifts the top flight', *Daily Telegraph*, 23 May.

'The most competitive English Premier League season for years', 26 April 2011. sporteconomist.blogspot.com/2011/04/most-competitive-english-premier-league.html

David Lacey, 2008. 'After the joy, the big battle begins', *Guardian*, 11 August.

Andrew Hodgson, 2009. '£150m on new stars puts Spurs in with big spenders', *London Evening Standard*, 10 November.

Matt Scott, 2010. 'Sheikh Mansour takes spending at Manchester City past half-billion mark', *Guardian*, 26 October.

A GREAT ADVERT FOR CRICKET: THE FA CUP

Niall Hickman, 1998. 'Arsenal win Euro vote on Wembley', *Daily Mail*, 20 July.

Jon Culley, 1999. 'United prepare to pull out of FA Cup', *Independent*, 29 June.

Kenny Dalglish, 2011. 'Survival or victory in the Cup? Sorry, there's only one winner and Houllier was spot on', *Daily Mail*, 6 March.

HAEMORRHAGING GRANDEUR AND GRAVITAS: EUROPEAN LEAGUES

Greatest Ever, 2007. *Greatest Ever Footballers*. Headline Publishing Group.

Amy Lawrence, 2008. 'Serie A on the b-list', *Guardian Sport Blog*, 23 November.

rsssf.com/miscellaneous/europa-poy.html

deloitte.com/view/en_GB/uk/industries/sportsbusinessgroup/sports/football/deloitte-football-money-league-2011/5596840c99e9d210VgnVCM2000001b56f00aRCRD.htm

ANOTHER FINE MESS: EUROPEAN COMPETITION

Phil Minshull, 2010. 'The great European Cup final of 1960 remembered', bbc.co.uk/blogs, 19 May.

Mark Ogden, 2005. 'United seeding plans thrown out', *Daily Telegraph*, 24 March.

Karolos Grohmann, 2011. 'Europa League is not my thing, says Bayern's Robben', *reuters.com*, 17 March.

Georgina Turner, 2011. 'Continental drift'. *When Saturday Comes*, Issue 293, July.

A BETRAYAL OF SMALL CHILDREN OF ALL AGES: INTERNATIONAL FOOTBALL

Simon Barnes, 2010. 'World Cup takes dive from the top', *The Times*, 17 July.

Gordon Farquhar, 2011. 'FIFA basks in $631 million profits', bbc.co.uk/blogs, 3 March.

'The greatest matches', *World Soccer Magazine*, July 2007.

Gary Payne, 2006. 'Winker will get kicking', *Sun*, 10 August.

CHAPTER FOUR

Georgina Turner, 2005. 'The fall and rise of Doncaster Rovers', guardian.co.uk/football, 30 November.

Sid Lowe, 2009. 'Are "madhouse" Atletico Madrid the worst run club in Europe?', *Guardian Sport Blog*, 3 November.

'One-on-one: Barry Fry', *FourFourTwo*, July 2009.

Crispin Northey, 2011. 'Forest Green ban burgers and sausages', *Stroud News & Journal*, 11 February.

leaguemanagers.com/managers/movers.html

'West Ham and Syd King', *East Ham Echo*, 27 April 1923.

FORGET IT, JAKE

David Conn, 2003. 'FA to devise "fit and proper person" test for directors', *Independent*, 16 August.

Ashling O'Connor, 2010. 'Fifa executive committee pair banned after investigation into corruption', *The Times*, 19 November.

Mike Collett, 2010. 'BBC makes new allegations against FIFA ex-co members', reuters.com, 29 November.

Paul Kelso, 2010. 'World Cup 2018: Spain-Portugal and Qatar could escape sanctions over bidding "collusion"', *Daily Telegraph*, 10 November.

Paul Kelso, 2010. 'Swiss government to investigate corruption in sports bodies in wake of FIFA decisions over World Cups', *Daily Telegraph*, 8 December.

David Conn, 2011. 'FIFA faces "watershed moment" for reform after corruptions allegations', guardian.co.uk/football, 29 May.

Owen Gibson, 2011. 'FIFA executives accused by former FA chairman Triesman of seeking bribes', guardian.co.uk/football, 10 May.

Leo Spall, 2010. 'FIFA say racism "not a factor" in battle for World Cup 2018', *MailOnline*, 4 September.

David Hills, 2011. 'Said & Done', *Observer*, 30 January.

'Serie A club Cagliari fined £22,010 after racist chanting aimed at Inter Milan striker Samuel Eto'o', *MailOnline*, 19 October 2010.

Tom Kington, 2010. 'Jose Mourinho suspended for three games and fined over handcuffs gesture', guardian.co.uk, 22 February.

David Hills, 2009. 'Said & Done', *Observer*, 22 February.

Barry Bearak, 2010. 'Cost of stadium reveals tensions in South Africa', *The New York Times*, March 12.

Barry Moody, 2010. 'FIFA launches 2,500 actions to protect World Cup brand', reuters.com, 6 May.

Peter Vinthagen Simpson, 2008. 'Borås loses out in UEFA burger battle', thelocal.se, 21 July.

THE GAME'S GONE SOFT

Diego Maradona, 2005. *El Diego: the autobiography of the world's greatest footballer.* Yellow Jersey Press.

ARE YOU THERE, GOD? IT'S ME, JEFF

'FIFA: Laws of the Game 2011/12'
fifa.com/mm/document/affederation/generic/81/42/36/lawsofthegame_2010_11_e.pdf

Jeff Winter, 2006. *Who's the B*****d in the black? Confessions of a Premiership referee.* Ebury Press.

CHAPTER FIVE

Emile Durkheim, 1912. *The Elementary Forms of Religious Life.* Oxford University Press.

Philip Banyard and Mark Shevlin, 2001. 'Responses of football fans to relegation of their team from the English Premier League: PTS?' *Irish Journal of Psychological Medicine*, 18(2): 66–7.

Mark Steels, 1994. 'Deliberate self poisoning – Nottingham Forest Football Club and FA Cup defeat', *Irish Journal of Psychological Medicine*, 11(2): 76–8.

Martin Thorpe, 1999. 'Diary', *Guardian*, 27 November.

Arthur Hopcraft, 1968. *The football man: people and passions in soccer.* Collins.

Nick Hornby, 1992. *Fever Pitch*. Gollancz.

Tim Crabbe, Adam Brown, Gavin Mellor and Kath O'Connor, 2006. *Football: an all consuming passion?* Substance.

STICKING IT TO THE FAN

Rogan Taylor, 1992. *Football and its fans: supporters and their relations with the game, 1885–1985*. Leicester University Press.

'FOOTBALL: COMMERCIAL ISSUES. A submission by the Football Task Force to the Minister for Sport', 22 December 1999.

Alan Hardaker, 1977. *Hardaker of the League*. Pelham Books.

David Conn, 1997. *The Football Business: fair game in the 90s?* Mainstream Publishing.

'Premier League club accounts: how in debt are they?'
guardian.co.uk/news/datablog/2011/may/19/football-club-accounts-debt

Nick Harris, 2010.'The Premier League: where the money went in 2009/10',
sportingintelligence.com, 16 May.

Nick Harris, 2009.'£1.78bn: record Premier League TV deal defies economic slump',
Independent, 7 February.

hansard.millbanksystems.com/lords/2002/jul/03/football-clubs

Manchester United, 2006. *The Official Manchester United Diary of the Season*. Orion.

Louise Taylor, 2011.'Niall Quinn "despises" Sunderland fans who watch foreign broadcasts',
Guardian, 4 February.

TAKE ME OUT TO THE BALL GAME

'Platini concedes Champions League final tickets are "too dear"', *Independent*, 21 April 2011.

football-league.co.uk/carlingcup/new/20110127/carling-cup-final-ticket-
details_2293330_2278000

'Luton Town fans angry at play-off final ticket prices', bbc.co.uk/news, 11 May 2011.

David Conn, 2011.'The Premier League has priced out fans, young and old',
guardian.co.uk, 16 August.

Stuart Rowson, 2011.'Clubs reveal all in BBC Sport Price of Football survey',
bbc.co.uk/sport, 1 August.

'QPR fans hit out at £72 ticket prices', mirrorfootball.co.uk, 25 May 2011.

SIT DOWN, SHUT UP

Vic Duke, 2002.'Local tradition versus globalisation: resistance to the McDonaldisation
and Disneyisation of Professional Football in England', *Football Studies*, 5(1): 5–23.

'Down the tunnel to disaster', *Guardian*, 17 April 1989.

Adam Brown (Ed.), 1998. *Fanatics! Power, identity and fandom in football*. Routledge.

'Open letter from Daniel Levy, chairman', tottenhamhotspur.com, 21 January 2011.

Anthony King, 1998. *The End of the Terraces*. Leicester University Press.

Jamie Cleland, 2010.'From passive to active: the changing relationship between supporters
and football clubs', *Soccer and Society* 11(5): 537–52.

CHAPTER SIX

Robert Milliken, 1996.'Sport is Murdoch's'battering ram'for pay TV', *Independent*, 16 October.

barb.co.uk

NO NEWS IS STILL NEWS

David James, 2011.'I was there at the birth of Sky Sports – and what a kerfuffle', *Observer*, 24 April.

'Real Madrid star Kaka: Man Utd boss Ferguson wanted to sign my brother and I', tribalfootball.com, 18 May 2011.

James Ducker, 2008.'Sir Alex Ferguson puts"Chelsea pensioners"under fire', *The Times*, 23 July.

David McDonnell, 2008.'Fergie taunts Scolari: you will never be as good as Mourinho', *Mirror*, 23 July.

Paul Doyle, 2011.'Tottenham tried to sign Luis Suárez but were told he was not up to it', *Guardian*, 13 May.

ABSOLUTE TWADDLE

Jeff Stelling, 2009. *Jelleyman's Thrown a Wobbly*. HarperCollins.

Gideon Haigh, 2011.'Ave Test cricket', ESPNcricinfo.com, 21 June.

Georgina Turner, 2011.'Partner in crime', *When Saturday Comes*, Issue 292, June.

Matt Lawton, 2009.'The best players of the world (and Xavi)', *Daily Mail*, 13 January.

'England"wilted under pressure"', bbc.co.uk/sport, 22 November 2007.

Geoffrey Green, 1953.'A new conception of football', *The Times*, 26 November.

Harry Redknapp, 2010.'Tactics don't win matches', *Sun*, 12 August

BELOW THE LINE

John Hudson, 2011.'Aaron Sorkin: What I read', theatlanticwire.com, 18 May.

Paul Hayward, 2011.'Juan Mata breaks the mechanics of Chelsea's pounding rhythms' (comments section), guardian.co.uk, 27 August.

Pamela Stephenson Connolly, 2011.'Am I in love with my mother?', guardian.co.uk, 28 July.

BALANCING THE BOOKS

FIFA, 2011.'IFAB agrees to one-year extension of Goal Line Technology tests', fifa.com, 5 March.

UEFA, 2011.'Clubs get share of Champions League revenue', uefa.com, 13 September.

Matt Hughes, 2009.'Eduardo da Silva wins appeal against ban for diving in Celtic match', *The Times*, 15 September.

Arthur Hopcraft, 1968. *The Football Man: people and passions in soccer*. Collins.

'Premier League agent fees to be published after FA strikes deal', guardian.co.uk/football, 15 July 2009.

'UEFA EXCO approves financial fair play', uefa.com, 21 September 2009.

Jonathan Wilson, 2011.'A tactical review of the 2010/11 season', *Guardian Sport Blog*, 7 June.

'Ticket trouble at the Bridge', fsf.org.uk, 16 September 2011.

INDEX

FC Bayern Munich 132, 135, 233
Beardsley, Peter 14
Beck, John 76
Beckenbauer, Franz 81
Beckham, David 31, 85, 87–8, 136
Belanov, Igor 135
Belgium football team 135
Bell, Laurie 52
Bellamy, Craig 88, 106
Belokon, Valeri 69
SL Benfica 28, 42, 103
Benítez, Rafael 67, 68–9, 102, 147, 224
Bent, Darren 112
Berbatov, Dimitar 78
Bergkamp, Dennis 207
Berthold, Thomas 41
Best, George 23, 28–9, 46–7, 117
Bilic, Slaven 212
bin Hammam, Mohammed 151
bin Zayed Al Nahyan, Sheikh Mansour 69, 104
Birmingham City FC 69, 107
Blackburn Rovers FC 13–14, 27, 97, 104, 106, 111, 170, 201
Blackpool FC 7, 18, 24, 60, 67–70, 78, 85, 107, 115, 155–6, 176, 189
Blanchflower, Danny 4, 23, 59, 221
Blatter, Sepp 111, 150, 152–3, 224, 231
Boateng, Kevin-Prince 77
Bolton Wanderers FC 6, 10, 27, 49, 60, 106, 111–2
Boniek, Zbigniew 76
Boruc, Artur 225
Bosman, Jean-Marc 36–7
Bowles, Stan 28
Bowyer, Ian 54
Brady, Liam 206
Brazil football team 5, 42, 57, 62, 71, 92, 133, 138, 139
Brehme, Andreas 42
Bremner, Billy 29–30, 113
Bridge, Wayne 32
Brighton and Hove Albion FC 62
Brooking, Trevor 40
Brown, Alan 226–7
Bruce, Steve 55, 147
Bruey, Stéphane 223
Buffon, Gianluigi 40
Bundesliga (German football league) 14, 103, 118, 132, 135, 179, 193, 232
Burns, Kenny 55

Busby, Sir Matt 2, 114
Busquets, Sergio 44
Butt, Nicky 85

C

Cagliari Calcio 153
Cambridge United FC 76
Cameroon football team 47, 90, 139
Campbell, D.J. 85
Campbell, Sol 49
Caniggia, Claudio 47
Cantona, Eric 145
Capello, Fabio 17, 107, 211
Cardiff FC 60, 106, 163
Carling Cup see League Cup
Carragher, Jamie 39
Carrick, Michael 214
Carroll, Andy 12–13
Carvalho, Ricardo 48, 49, 84
Celtic FC 84, 102, 124–7
    see also Scottish Premier League
Centenaro, Michele 228
César, Júlio 93, 121
chairmen, club see individuals by name; owners and chairmen, club
Champions League 10, 16, 19, 37, 43, 44, 60, 64, 66–9, 72, 75, 83–5, 99, 102, 104, 111–12, 116, 118–9, 121, 124, 127–32, 135, 146, 155, 178, 180, 183–4, 204, 211, 214, 223–5, 228, 230, 233–4
    see also European Cup
    see
Championship see Football League
Charity Shield 29
Charles, John 3–4
Charlton, Bobby 33
Chelsea FC 13, 14, 16, 18, 27, 36, 45, 48, 51, 52, 63, 65, 67, 75, 79–80, 83, 100, 102, 114, 115, 120, 146, 157, 197, 205, 233–4
Chimbonda, Pascal 41
US Città di Palermo 144
Claridge, Steve 76
Clough, Brian 25, 29, 53–4, 105, 148, 218, 224, 226
Cohen, George 33
Colchester United FC 113
Cole, Ashley 18, 29, 32, 222
Cole, Joe 37, 75
Collymore, Stan 52
Cologne FC 49, 54
commentators and pundits 195–6, 206–11

INDEX